Saltwater Chronicles

Notes on Everything Under the Nova Scotia Sun

LESLEY CHOYCE

NIMBUS
PUBLISHING
— NIMBUS.CA —

Nimbus Publishing Limited
3660 Strawberry Hill St, Halifax, NS, B3K 5A9
(902) 455-4286 nimbus.ca

Printed and bound in Canada

NB1439

Editor: Angela Mombourquette
Cover design: Peggy Issenman, Peggy & Co.
Interior design: Rudi Tusek
Cover photo: iStockphoto.com (shaunl)

Library and Archives Canada Cataloguing in Publication

Title: Saltwater chronicles : notes on everything under the Nova Scotia sun / Lesley Choyce.
Names: Choyce, Lesley, 1951- author.
Identifiers: Canadiana (print) 20200162055 | Canadiana (ebook) 20200162098 | ISBN 9781771088268 (softcover) | ISBN 9781771088275 (HTML)
Subjects: LCSH: Choyce, Lesley, 1951- | LCSH: Authors, Canadian—20th century—Biography. | LCSH: Nova Scotia—Anecdotes. | LCGFT: Autobiographies.
Classification: LCC PS8555.H668 Z46 2020 | DDC C818/.5409—dc23

Nimbus Publishing acknowledges the financial support for its publishing activities from the Government of Canada, the Canada Council for the Arts, and from the Province of Nova Scotia. We are pleased to work in partnership with the Province of Nova Scotia to develop and promote our creative industries for the benefit of all Nova Scotians.

For Linda, Pamela, and Sunyata

CONTENTS

INTRODUCTION

IF I HAD NOT BEEN A SURFER, I PROBABLY WOULD NOT HAVE MOVED
to Nova Scotia. If I had not dropped out of graduate school in
Manhattan and quit my teaching job in New York City in 1978, I
would have missed out on many adventures. Perhaps there would
have been urban exploits to keep me satisfied, but I had chosen
a rural life by the sea on the North Atlantic coast of Canada. And
that has made all the difference.

Mainland Nova Scotia is nearly an island. The fierce and ever-
changing Atlantic is to the south and west. The Northumberland
Strait and the Gulf of St. Lawrence are roughly to the north, and
the famously fluctuating Bay of Fundy separates most of the province from the rest of continental North America. The Isthmus of
Chignecto, a mere twenty-four kilometres wide, tethers the province to New Brunswick. It is mostly tidal estuaries and grassy
lowlands and, thanks to global climate change and rising sea levels, it will one day be flooded and Nova Scotia will become a true
island, surrounded on all sides by water.

We do already have, however, thirty-eight hundred
coastal islands, some with exotic names like Shagroost, Tickle,
Brokenback, Hog, Rum, Boot, Chockle Cap, Roaring Bull, and

Frying Pan Islands. I have even explored some, but not nearly all, of them. For forty years I have lived a coastal life, waking each day to look across a saltwater lake toward the sea. I've grown to understand the ever-changing winds and tides, the calm summer mornings, and the fierce midnight winter storms.

I am a writer by trade and I once wrote a history of the province called *Nova Scotia: Shaped by the Sea.* The land and the people of this province have shaped me as well. The sea and the soul of this place have washed over and around me and have made me who I am today. *Saltwater Chronicles* is the story of my geography, and the chapters herein create a topographical map of one man at a certain time and place.

To be precise, the locale is Lawrencetown Beach, Nova Scotia, with forays into the big city of Halifax; the time runs into the past, and into the web of my beliefs, opinions, and imagination. The stories are true, and whatever wisdom may be present was hard-earned. There is good news and bad news here and it is only worth reading if I have done the proper ancient job of telling a good tale.

You may be shocked to discover that these chapters, in many ways, celebrate the ordinary. Life's big lesson for me, these days, seems to be all about discovering the extraordinary in the ordinary and then keeping track of the story to share it with others. I believe in the life lived, not the life observed. But then, don't we all? It's just that we so easily get distracted.

I'm not new to autobiography. I've published five previous books that have chronicled my life at various stages. The first, *An Avalanche of Ocean,* came out in 1987. It was followed by *Transcendental Anarchy, Driving Minnie's Piano, How to Fix Your Head,* and *Seven Ravens.*

The years explored in *Saltwater Chronicles* are 2014 through 2017. Given that I was born in 1951, that means it covers my life from ages sixty-three through sixty-six. The ambitious, idealistic, and somewhat arrogant young man inside me is still alive and kicking while the old man ahead is beckoning me forward with a malicious grin.

I'm aware of the audacity of this all—a man telling tales about his everyday life to readers he has likely never met. But for some strange reason, I feel compelled to tell you what it's like for a lifetime surfer to turn sixty-five; to regale you with stories about reading, walking, napping, and the subconscious mind. I am convinced you will want to hear about the perils of coastal gardening, winter snow, potholes, short attention spans, and about the foods I ate as a kid.

You'll note that I am still pissed off that Jimmy Buffet stole my best wetsuit boots, but that I was ecstatic to be part of a rescue team to save a 180-kilogram sunfish beached during a raging storm. Along the way I have fallen into wells and adapted to the crisis of becoming a respectable citizen. During the four years covered here, I have experienced the death of my father and of my family dog. I have helped my wife through cancer, and together we have navigated the North Atlantic waves both literal and metaphorical. Through it all, I have recorded a most human range of sorrows and joys. All of it ordinary and yet extraordinary at the same time.

Welcome to the chronicles of my saltwater life.

Lesley Choyce
Lawrencetown Beach, Nova Scotia, Canada
January 4, 2020

A SURFER TURNS SIXTY-FIVE

LAST YEAR, AS MY SIXTY-FOURTH BIRTHDAY WAS APPROACHING, I started writing an article called "When I'm Sixty-Four," thinking I was rather clever by borrowing the title from the Beatles song. Like a multitude of other men and women of my generation, I was both pleased and appalled at the fact that I was approaching this unimaginable milestone. The only problem was that I discovered a fistful of other articles in newspapers and magazines by other clever birthday men and women who had already written pieces with that borrowed title. So I decided not to write at all.

I continued to ponder my mortality as the pages of the calendar flipped by and, lo and behold, in the merry month of March I turned sixty-five. I figured it was time to write about this blessed-slash-cursed (and inevitable) event.

I must say—things move fast at this age. Do you remember when you were young and the summers seemed to last forever? That was a wonderful thing and it meant that once you were out of school in June, you had a hell of a long run until that day of doom returned in September. Alas, summers go by quickly now. Days are way too short and seasons pass like the wind. It's like

I've slipped into an alternate universe where everything is on fast-forward.

It's only when I am stuck in uncomfortable social situations or in tedious meetings that time seems to grind to a halt and minutes slip slowly and grudgingly by. If anyone has discovered a better means of slowing time down so we can savour each ecstatic moment, please drop me a line before I'm too old to appreciate it.

One more observation about time and aging: I swear to you it seems like yesterday that I was sitting in a grade seven French class hearing my teacher drone on about verb conjugations while I was daydreaming about girls or surfing (or probably both). And then, I kid you not, within a wasp's blink of an eye, I discovered I was sixty-five years old and writing about, well, turning sixty-five. It all happened so quickly. If it hasn't happened to you yet, I suggest you slow things down as best you can and live every moment to the fullest.

Age is a funny thing. When I was a kid, I naturally believed that people who were in their thirties, like my parents, were old. Grandparents, in their sixties, were *really* old. My grandfather was still farming, however, and travelling about North America in his Oldsmobile with my grandmother. We called him "Gaga" because my older brother had lovingly mispronounced his name as a baby and the name had somehow stuck. (I am glad he wasn't around when Lady Gaga came on the scene. Such a unique name should not have fallen from grace like that.)

My grandfather would put four teaspoons of sugar into a glass of iced tea. He ate a lot of raw oysters, and he enjoyed watching TV westerns like *Gunsmoke, Bonanza,* and *Maverick* while lying down on the "chesterfield." That odd combination of diet and entertainment is what I believe helped him live past ninety. I learned about real aging by hanging around with him during his final years and recording his stories of the First World War. His memory of the war was much more vivid to him than the memory of anything he'd done in recent weeks, so I learned then and there another lesson about the relativity of time and memory.

So here I am, in my mid-sixties, receiving notices in the mail from the federal government about old-age pensions, and letters of apology from the premier about screwing around with the Seniors' Pharmacare Program. That letter, by the way, reminded me of one I'd had to write when I was a kid. My friend Dan had convinced me it would be "tons of fun" to buy a dozen eggs and throw them at the side of a house owned by a mean "old" (probably thirty-five-year-old) man who lived in the neighbourhood. Someone saw us do it, however, and told the guy, who then called my mother. My mom made me use my writing skills (pretty good, even then) to send an apology. And I did just that, saying that what we had done was "unkind" and "inappropriate." I had forgotten about that letter until Stephen McNeil's apology arrived; it said he'd had second thoughts on pharmacare changes. He even added, "I also want to apologize for a letter you may have received about the program. The letter was inappropriate." I felt a kinship to him as I read it, recalling my own embarrassment over the egg incident.

So I should feel cheery about seniors' discounts and the possibility of young people giving up their seats for me on the bus. But those things bring little joy into my aging heart.

Two summers ago, somebody organized a photo shoot of a bunch of us Nova Scotia surfers over sixty. In the invitation to the photo-op, another photo, taken circa 1976, was emailed around and there we were: long hair, sideburns, standing on the beach with our surfboards, gleaming with youth. As of 2015, many of us still surfed and, as we gathered for the second photo of the "before and after" sequence, I admit we were a fairly healthy lot. Surfers tend to age gracefully, in case you didn't know. We joked and laughed and reminisced, but I left the scene feeling a little funny. Why did I feel so mournful?

Well, I guess it just has to do with a haunting grief that we feel when we recognize that a certain phase of our life is solidly behind us. We grieve over the fact that we lived it once and now it is gone. It's more than that, but it is a form of sadness that verges on the inexpressible. To try to nail it down, I think it goes like this: most of us have had a whole lot of really great, truly well-lived moments in our lives and we wish we could live them over again and again.

But aside from reliving them in memory, we can't.

So we find ourselves another year older and we wonder, yet again—how did we get here?

What does it mean when a *surfer* turns sixty-five? For one thing, I hadn't surfed as much during the previous two winters as I had in the years before. The winter of 2015 was a cruel, heartless one, but last winter was mild by comparison. I had been out of the water for more than a month when a shockingly mild February 27 rolled around. It was sunny, relatively warm, and I spied a jaw-dropping five-foot hollow wave breaking on the rocky shores of a nearby point of land on the Eastern Shore.

My wife, Linda, tucked me into my winter surfing gear—an unflattering drysuit that makes me look a bit like a cross between an astronaut and Santa Claus—that makes winter surfing tolerable. I drove to the headland and paddled out into the sea. I felt the warmth of the sun on my face and I scooped up a paw full of salt water and swished it around in my mouth.

When a set of waves came my way, I dug deep, sucked powerful gulps of fresh salty air into my lungs, and dropped down the gleaming face of the cleanest, most perfect wave I'd seen all winter. If you were on the shoreline, it probably didn't even look all that dramatic, really. My own moves were undoubtedly not all that graceful, and the wave probably lasted seconds, not minutes.

Yet, for however long it was, time stood still. I was neither young nor old. I was more spirit than flesh, or so I believed, six-and-a-half decades into this life.

There were more waves after that, more transcendental moments. Those waves spoke to me and they reminded me that mere numbers added to your age mean very little. It felt good to be alive—and I had a hunch there would be many more moments like this to be lived before the clock stops ticking.

ISLANDS OF THE HEART

IN 1978 I GAVE UP CITY LIFE TO LIVE BY THE SEA AT LAWRENCETOWN Beach in Nova Scotia, where I could write and surf and ramble and breathe in sweet salty air. On summer days, I'd paddle an old beat-up canoe with my two young daughters, Sunyata and Pamela, across the tidal waters of Lawrencetown Lake. We'd land on an uninhabited island where we'd visit an abandoned cabin with battered beds, mouldy walls, and leftover kitchen utensils. Humans had given up on the place and porcupines had moved in. Apparently, they lived in the rafters, because in the centre of the cabin sat a knee-high pile of porcupine poop. But that wasn't the most intriguing feature of the place.

Instead, it was the dozen or so magazine photos of Elvis Presley tacked up on the bare walls. Sunyata suggested this must have been where Elvis Presley had been hiding after most of his fans had thought him dead. In fact, it was obvious Elvis had adopted several porcupines to live inside the cabin with him as pets and, when Elvis moved on, the porcupines had remained in the famous singer's hideout. Hence we named the spot "Elvis Island."

It's not the only island in our vicinity. A couple of miles off the coast at Lawrencetown lies Shut-in Island, a barren, rugged,

6

lonely bit of rock and sand. In the early nineteenth century, a man named John Harris lived there. A tough, solitary, but enterprising old Bluenoser, he was a ship pilot by trade. His lonely outpost allowed him to keep an eye out for sailing ships bound for Halifax. Then he'd row his dory out into the blustery expanse of the North Atlantic and offer his services, guiding the captains safely into port, before rowing himself back the many miles to his island home. One can only vaguely begin to comprehend what a life that must have been.

It is said this island is haunted by the spirit of the old sea dog because, on moonlit nights, you can see a light coming from Shut-in Island—the light once seen from shore in the days when the sea pilot had lived his lonely life there.

One calm summer day I decided to knee-paddle an old windsurfer to the island just to see what it would be like to be alone at sea on a small craft, with nothing but my arms and wits to get me there and home. I also wanted to discover whether there was anything unusual about the island. I guess I wanted to see if it was haunted.

About a mile out to sea my mind started to grab onto some basic facts. I was far from shore and no one even knew I was on this whimsical quest. It's funny how quickly things change when you are alone in the vast expanse of the ocean. I wondered what would happen if anything went wrong. I pondered what I was doing out here. Suddenly I was having a hard time keeping my balance.

That's when I heard the sound. Something behind me, some creature of the deep, had leapt from the water and fallen back in with a loud, low *ker-whump*. I felt a small wave wobble my frail craft. I looked back but saw nothing except the ripples it left behind.

I paddled a little faster. Shut-in Island still seemed a long way off.

It happened a second time, then a third—but each time I turned to look, I saw nothing. Whatever it was, it was quite large. And it was following me.

Logic insisted it was a very large seal. But logic was not the ruler in my brain. I paddled on, breathing just a bit harder. A sea breeze was stirring and I knew the conditions could change quickly. The island was another twenty minutes away and I decided I would at least land, do my reconnaissance, and head back. I didn't keep looking back to determine whether it was a seal, fearing that if I actually saw the beast and determined it was not…well, you know.

My knees ached as I waded ashore and surveyed the pebbly sand and sea oats, wild peas and roses, and two acres of land that had been whitewashed by the droppings of thousands of gulls. I walked, wobbly, to the centre of the island and saw for myself the source of Shut-in's haunted light: there was a small saltwater pond, sprouting cattails and sporting algae-covered rocks. On moonlit nights, I supposed, the light would strike the pool and bounce back, making it look like a light source itself. So much for one stubborn mystery.

By then, the rising south wind was ruffling my hair, and the mainland looked a long, long way off. I began my paddle shoreward, feeling more haunted than when I began, reflecting all the while on what men had felt like before me—alone at sea, keeping fear at bay, rowing or paddling—whatever it took to keep moving forward—heading home to the safety of the mainland shore.

NOT FAR FROM SHUT-IN IS Wedge Island. Because it's barely tethered to the mainland, you can walk there at low tide. In early summer, hundreds of gulls swirl around as you gingerly hike along the top of the high wedge of land that gets more narrow with every passing year, thanks to the relentless pounding of storm waves. Gull nests with hatched babies—puffy brown creatures who look nothing like adult gulls—rest in the high grasses. The parents chastise you from above as you take care to avoid disturbing the young ones by arcing around the hatching sites, walking seaward until you come to a most curious old well.

A family had a farm out here long ago, on fields now fully swallowed by the sea. But the well is still there, filled to the brim with fresh water, its stone walls a mere three feet from the side of a thirty-foot cliff. As I sit and study it, I realize the sea will soon eat away what is left of the land, and the well, with its deep, dark fresh water, will spill into the sea.

From here, looking west, is an even more desolate island known as Rat Rock. It is home to many massive seals who lie on the exposed rocks at sunset and make the most beautiful, ethereal, and haunting sounds I've ever heard.

I think of islands as places of pilgrimage; places of refuge—each one an independent nation of itself, alive and unique, the best of them pure and uncorrupted. These islands dream the dreams of green moss and orange lichen and sometimes hundred-year-old stunted black spruce, living in bogs and looking barely alive in their own ragged beauty.

I recently opened a 1928 gazetteer of place names in Nova Scotia and charted the names of the myriad islands around this province. Each name seemed to have its own story.

There is Cuckold Rock and Brother Rocks, Potters Ledge, Isle Haute, Solomon's Island, Half Bald Tusket Island, Devils Limb and Devils Island, Pumpkin Island, Bear Point, Thrum Cap, Murder Island, Egg Island, Western Shagroost, Tickle Island, Brokenback Island, St. Peters Island, St. Paul Island, Shag Rock, Hog Island, Rum Island, Boot Island, Quaker Island, Chockle Cap, Burnt Island, Betty Island, Roaring Bull, and Frying Pan Island. And thousands more.

Every stone on the shore of those islands has a story that reaches back thousands, or perhaps millions, of years. In summer, tiny red spiders live among these stones. There are gulls in the sky, plovers on the sand, and sea ducks in the waters nearby. Every time I set foot on an uninhabited island, I feel myself pulled back in time. I feel pleasantly disconnected from civilization and all the trivial things of civilized life. I smell the sweet cocktail of rotting kelp and salt air. I sense the sacredness of such places.

The daughters who ventured to Elvis Island with me are now grown up, and I have a five-year-old grandson named Aidan. He, perhaps, will have children and they will have children who grow up in a heavily populated, highly technological and artificial world. I'd like to leave them some kind of a message asking them to seek out my islands and others—east and west, north and south.

Because when we find our way to those real islands (or to the imagined ones) we journey there to leave the crowd, to leave the madness, to be apart, to reflect, to ponder, to meditate, to pray, to celebrate what is within and what the island gives us. We cross deep waters, we face challenges, and we walk ashore—waiting for the gifts these islands offer.

HOW READING SHAPES A LIFE

To BEGIN AT THE BEGINNING, I THINK MY MOTHER READ NURSERY rhymes to me when I was very young, so I wasn't the one actually doing the reading. But I guess this is how most of us start out. She would have read from a really old traditional book of English rhyming poems such as "London Bridge is Falling Down," "Little Jack Horner," "Humpty Dumpty," and "Little Tommy Tucker." I was too young to question the absurdity of these poetic morsels or their irrelevance to my twentieth-century life. Like most kids at that stage, I was just happy to have my mom reading to me.

My own attempts at reading would occur before I made my way to school, and I suspect I was faking it—looking at the pictures and pretending to read the large printed words on the page. But, hey, isn't that how most of us learn almost everything we do? We fake it for a while until we really figure it out, and then learn it little by little until we are no longer faking it but doing the real thing.

Thanks to the invention (and intervention) of television into our lives, as a little kid I was thrust into the Disneyfied world of books and their characters: Cinderella, Pinocchio, Paul Bunyan, and, of course, characters like Mickey Mouse, Donald Duck, Pecos

Bill, and the like. I had a proud little collection of Golden Books and I think that, with my mother's help, I actually started to read real words (again, the pictures helped). These were what we call in the publishing business "board books," with really thick cardboard pages and shiny coating—books that kids and dogs could chew and they would still be serviceable.

By the time I was five, school began to get in the way of my homemade education and, like millions of other North American children, I was introduced to the even more absurd, totally mundane antics of the ultra-famous Dick and Jane. "Why Dick and why Jane?" I pondered by the time I was six. *Fun With Dick and Jane* was really not that much fun at all, and, truth be told, the kids in the books looked really dated and boring to us tiny hipsters in the early 1960s.

I was much more interested in the oddball antics in Dr. Seuss books: *The Cat in the Hat, How the Grinch Stole Christmas!,* and *Horton Hatches the Egg.* But *Bartholomew and the Oobleck* was definitely my favourite (I never read another oobleck book that came even close to that one).

Around that time I also had a new-found obsession with yet another Disney re-creation: the historical character Davy Crockett. TV had set it in motion, but I had Davy Crockett books that I read over and over, often while wearing a genuine Davy Crockett "coonskin" cap made from real raccoon fur (my grandmother Minnie had sacrificed her old raccoon coat from the "roaring" 1920s to meticulously stitch it together for me). I'm pretty sure I also had my trusty Mattel Davy Crockett replica rifle, Old Betsy, by my side. I know it seems odd to think of a child reading while holding a gun, but you have to remember that this was an American childhood.

You don't fully realize it when you're a kid, but reading—no matter what you are reading—is a meditative act. You sit alone with words on a page and you transport yourself into other lives, real or imagined, and other worlds—worlds you could never conceive of on your own.

As I grew, I continued to read, and it helped shape who I became.

By the time I was setting the Crockett books and the coonskin cap aside, my mother had introduced me to the public library. Our town didn't have one and we had to drive a fair distance to visit a real library—an old one that housed tiers of books from floor to second-storey ceiling, complete with spiral wrought-iron staircases and narrow, thrilling catwalks that were lined with books.

I must have had grandiose notions about my intellectual abilities because, with my trusty new library card in hand, I was checking out adult books on rocks and minerals, ornithology, space travel, Formula One race cars, and military history. I especially liked books that were heavy in weight and hard to reach, from higher shelves. I did sometimes just look at the pictures but prided myself, with a dictionary nearby, in trying to learn the meanings of words that appeared on these important pages. I especially liked learning new military terms—words like flame-thrower, rocket grenade, howitzer, battle cruiser, and thermonuclear device. Later, as an anti-war activist in the early 1970s, I pondered my childhood fascination with weaponry and war, but I concluded the reading had not seriously damaged me, and maybe it had even somehow shaped my later opinions on the subject.

By the time I was twelve, I had discovered that by mailing away to government agencies I could receive free brochures and booklets about a wide range of subjects, from home safety to corn farming to nuclear energy. It was the latter that most interested me and I was a voracious reader of propaganda about how "atomic energy" was going to pave the way to a great future for us all. My favourite booklet was titled *Meet Citizen Atom—Your Partner in Progress.*

My teachers thought my preference for reading materials was a bit odd, to say the least, and more than one tried to steer me into the school library to read "books more suitable for my age." I was introduced to a series of blue-green hardback biographies of people like Joe DiMaggio, Ted Williams, and Babe Ruth. Little did I know these were watered-down versions of the real (and sometimes sordid) lives of famous sports figures. This was the trouble with a school library and its contents. In the Bambino's bowdlerized biography, for example, there was not a word spilled about his drinking and womanizing—only his baseball heroics.

I instinctively knew there was something wrong with reading books considered appropriate for young teenagers and drifted away from approved reading into the more intriguing world of science fiction. My mother took me to used bookstores, where she would buy dozens of paperback copies of mysteries by Erle Stanley Gardner and Agatha Christie for herself, and I would purchase used ten-cent copies of novels by Jules Verne, H. G. Wells, and A. E. van Vogt. Some even had cheesy, lurid covers with images of nearly naked women struggling with aliens—images that had almost nothing to do with the story. Jules Verne was my favourite science fiction author in those days, and I remember reading a rather lengthy *Journey to the Center of the Earth* cover to cover. Not long after I finished reading the novel, I discovered Hollywood had come out with a movie version starring James

Mason and Pat Boone. But the movie version was nothing like the real thing. No surprises there.

I eventually moved on to more contemporary science fiction writers like Robert A. Heinlein, Kurt Vonnegut Jr., Ray Bradbury, and Harlan Ellison. They inspired me to start writing my own outrageous and slightly ridiculous science fiction stories. I also dabbled in poetry, having been misinformed by books and movies that writing poetry would make girls like you.

Inevitably, I began to read outside of the science fiction ghetto, and I was introduced to J. D. Salinger's *The Catcher in the Rye,* William Golding's *Lord of the Flies, Johnnie Got His Gun* by Dalton Trumbo and *One Flew Over the Cuckoo's Nest* by Ken Kesey. In high school I was forced to read a number of truly dull novels that nearly threw me off my reading game, but by the time I hit university, the gates of literary paradise swung wide open. Heinlein's *Stranger in a Strange Land* startled me. Ken Kesey's *Sometimes a Great Notion* entranced me. Jack Kerouac's *On the Road* set me off on a hitchhiking frenzy across the country. Tom Wolfe's *The Electric Kool-Aid Acid Test* suggested I was leading a pretty sheltered existence, and Baba Ram Dass's *Be Here Now* and Alan Watts's *The Way of Zen* clearly pointed out I had been living inside a Western cultural prison that constrained my spirit and intellect—and it was time to set myself free.

There is so much more to report about those days, but suffice it to say: books changed my life. So I decided to become a writer, and I proceeded to see more than ninety of my books published by 2017. I never know if I am writing a good book or a mediocre one, but I always give it my best shot. I admit that I have written a couple of not-so-great books along the way, but that was all part of the learning curve. Of course, I continue to read, and whenever

I discover a truly great book I am inspired to attempt to write one that is just as good.

So I'm sure that, in the long run, good writing and a good story will not only survive—but prevail.

IN PRAISE OF NAPPING

I THINK A LOT OF THE WORLD'S PROBLEMS COULD BE SOLVED IF people took more naps. I don't always have the luxury of taking an afternoon nap, but when I do I awake refreshed, renewed, and revitalized. I feel certain that if more of us partook of this ancient holy ritual, humans would do less damage to this already maligned planet—and might find the inner strength and wisdom necessary to carry humanity through this already perilous century.

Fortunately for me, I inherited the napping gene from my father. Most days he worked hard, rising at 5:30 A.M. to head off into the dark morning to prepare diesel trucks for their daily operations. By the time he arrived home nearly ten hours later, he loved nothing more than to plant himself in the La-Z-Boy and sleep for about twenty to thirty minutes before my mother put our home-cooked dinner on the kitchen table. My father's greatest skill regarding daytime sleeping was his ability to almost automatically fall asleep. The procedure had merely four steps: 1. Sit down. 2. Put feet up. 3. Close eyes. 4. Fall into a deep sleep. Bingo.

The TV could be on full blast, my mom could be banging pots around in the kitchen, and the dog could be barking as well.

But none of this interfered with his nap. At the time, because I was just a child, I suppose I didn't quite see the point. But now I see things differently: I am a convert to the wisdom of napping.

As I grew older, I discovered I could fall asleep on buses, planes, in airports, and occasionally during university lectures on proper bibliographic form. Through a number of years when I had a so-called regular job, I discovered—to my chagrin—that there was no room in which I could nap during the working day. Bosses were not paying one bit of attention to all the research about how napping makes one more productive. No sirree! An employee was expected to remain fully awake while employed. How absurd was that?

One summer, however, I did have a job that permitted napping. I was loading tractor-trailers on the graveyard shift and, when we took our break—"lunch" we called it—at 1:00 A.M., many of us ate a quick liverwurst sandwich and then fell asleep sitting upright on an uncomfortable vinyl sofa in the break room. By 2:00 A.M. we would be rudely awakened by our boss, Big Clarence, and told to go back to loading freight on trucks. Although the naps were generally helpful, the rude awakenings were no fun at all.

But I am mostly referring here to the classic nap. It should take place somewhere between one and three o'clock in the afternoon and it should last between twenty and thirty minutes. Any more than that and you're likely to fall into a deeper sleep, which will leave you groggy when you wake up. If I had my way, the right to nap would be enshrined in the Canadian Charter of Rights and Freedoms and in the UN's Universal Declaration of Human Rights.

Ideally, one should nap on a sofa in a warm, sunlit room. The napping genes gifted to me by my dad allow me to nap while the TV is on, or even while other people are in the room discussing income taxes, politics, restaurants, or their vacations in Florida. The trick is to close your eyes and, if possible, stop worrying about all your obligations and responsibilities. If all goes well, you might even leave your body—metaphorically speaking, of course.

The wise and well-rested folks at the National Sleep Foundation in the US point out that "naps can restore alertness, enhance performance, and reduce mistakes and accidents." Apparently, NASA did a study on napping and determined that a forty-minute nap can do wonders. NASA's researchers found that, after a snooze, astronaut performance was up by 34 percent, and the astronauts were a whopping 100 percent more alert. (Forty minutes seems a tad long to this pro napper but I won't quibble with NASA, since an afternoon in their employ may involve repairing an orbiting space station or planning an eventual trip to Mars, whereas my own afternoon responsibilities may simply involve letting the dog out to pee or driving to the end of the road to pick up the mail.)

And, apparently, there's money to be made from napping. Fifty-eight-year-old Constance Kobylarz Wilde of Mountain View, California, who has apparently made a name for herself as a highly successful "health blogger," says she owes much of her success to the fifteen-to-twenty–minute nap. She is only one of a legion of professionals advocating the power of the short daytime sleep. I'm not sure what a health blogger does during the course of a day, but I'm sure it is very important. When I was growing up, my high school guidance counsellor never suggested that health blogging would be a viable profession during my lifetime. Instead, as you'll read later in "The Road Not Taken," he actually gave me a test that determined I should become a coal miner because of my interest in rocks.

Nonetheless, my point is that napping may not be such an old-fashioned idea if Ms. Wilde and other people with very contemporary professions like health blogging are embracing it.

There's really no downside to napping. Maybe some people are afraid that they might miss something important when they are zoned out—but it seems unlikely. My advice: turn off your laptop, iPhone, and anything else that dings when you have an incoming message from Facebook or Twitter, then sit back and close your eyes. Those selfies and funny pictures of really old people smoking weed—or whatever—will still be there when you wake up.

BOOGIE BOARDING WITH CANCER

IN THE EARLY MONTHS OF OUR RELATIONSHIP, LINDA ANNOUNCED one sunny spring afternoon that she might have cancer. Life had had its ups and downs for me over the previous couple of years, but this was a new twist. I managed to maintain a pretty good non-reaction reaction, which is to say I sat silently at first and tried not to show shock or fear—or any sign that might indicate that I might quickly decide it was a good time to run for the hills before the going got rough.

Maybe Linda thought my silence was a bad sign; she diplomatically offered me a chance to opt out of the relationship. "If you decide you want to maybe bow out now, I'd understand," she said. In truth, if someone was to look objectively at things, a guy might do just that. Knowing that he was likely in for a long, traumatic ordeal that could end badly, why not just get out while the getting was good?

As it turned out, my upbringing, my growing love for this woman, and my adult attachment to everything I learned in Boy Scouts would not allow that. I smiled what I hoped was a soft, sad smile and simply said, "I'm in." And so began our mutual adventure with cancer.

I know—adventure is not exactly the right word. I don't even know what the right word is. I know for sure it was not a "fight." We were not about to combat cancer, nor were we about to give in to it. I think it was more like giving over to it. We would work with the experience and, with the guidance of modern medicine and good advice, see what we could learn from the shared experience.

Everyone's trip down cancer alley is a bit different, but some things are universal. There are tests and blood work, and, of course, there is learning about the disease.

Linda's brand of cancer was non-Hodgkin's lymphoma. I'd heard of it, but that was about all. Linda's hematologist told her: "If you have to have cancer, this is the one you want." The good news was that it was treatable. The bad news, she said, was that after treatment there was a good chance it would come back. I think, once this was made clear to me, Linda offered me a second opportunity to bail out. But by that point, I had already envisioned myself as chief cancer-coach-and-shoulder-to-lean-on. We would see this thing through.

The treatment would be chemotherapy, a word that has never put a smile on anyone's face. We were told that Linda would likely lose her hair. At the Victoria Building (part of the QEII Health Sciences Centre) we were sent up for a tour of the "Sunshine Room," where free wigs could be had. No offence to the good and cheerful people who volunteer to host cancer patients there, but we found it a tad too depressing. I think it might just have been that the idea of trying to put a smiley face on cancer, chemo, and hair loss just didn't sit well with us. None of the wigs seemed quite right—they all looked like the kinds of wigs that say to the world: "I have cancer and I'm wearing this wig." We nearly bolted down the stairs from there.

A while later, I took it upon myself to go wig shopping while I was in the US. The wig store I chose was crowded with mostly Black and Hispanic women, and it had really great wigs. I tried them on and asked the people in the store for advice. They were friendly and responsive, and more than one must have assumed I was a cross-dresser. "Honey, that is just not you," one older Puerto Rican woman said to me. I particularly liked some of the really long, dark wigs that made me look like a member of KISS or some other 1980s rock band.

In the end, I settled on two: a cheap wig and an expensive one. The cheap one was synthetic and had a kind of sex worker look, but I figured it was good enough to wear around the house. The expensive one was made from real hair and had a movie-star aura about it. (Later, after watching comedian Chris Rock's documentary *Good Hair*, I would feel guilty about buying something made from the hair of an impoverished woman in India.) The young woman at the register told me I had made good decisions and wished me well with my new hair.

The advice from the hospital and the hair specialist was that once the treatments have started and the hair starts falling out in clumps, people freak out, so it's better to just cut it all off at once and be done with it.

Linda and I disagreed with that advice. In the end she lost some, but not all, of her hair, so the wigs ended up sitting permanently on the Styrofoam heads, only to be brought out at Halloween.

I had gone with Linda to several sessions with the hematologist and we had done some of our own research, so we were about to go into the chemo phase with our eyes wide open. Just before the treatments were to begin, we headed off to Yorkshire,

England, to share some good times in the English countryside before things got tough.

After our travels, Linda went back to her job as principal at Citadel High School. The first step for Linda in her chemo would be to have a "PowerPort" (a central venous catheter) surgically implanted in her chest. This would stay in place until all the treatments were over; it would make the injections easier and the ordeal somewhat less painful. She had determined she wanted to go on her own to the hospital for that procedure, so when the day came, she walked from the school to the Victoria Building. All went seemingly well, and she walked back to school.

As soon as Linda walked into the office, the vice-principals realized she was high on the painkillers that had been pumped into her for the operation. She was in a jolly good mood—and anxious to share some thoughts with the student body over the PA system.

I'm sure the kids would have loved it, but, fortunately, the more sober administrators kept her behind closed doors in her office until the drugs wore off and I rolled around to pick her up after the final bell.

Linda headed into the chemo treatment—which lasted over six months and was followed by another two years of follow-up treatments—as I educated myself on how to be a good cancer coach. I soon realized that my most important job was to keep a good attitude and to promote the same in Linda, no matter how rough things got.

Spending time around hospitals, we learned what most people learn: that there is a lot of waiting involved. Nonetheless, everyone we encountered at the hospital was professional, caring, and kind.

On a chemo day, I'd drive Linda to the hospital and she'd

usually start to feel the first wave of anxiety while crossing the MacKay Bridge from Dartmouth into Halifax. She didn't have to say it outright but her emotional state came across loud and clear as we came off the bridge and headed south down the peninsula. *I don't want to do this* was what she was thinking as we got bogged down in traffic. I'd try to keep her distracted by telling her a story—anything I could think of to get her mind off the day ahead.

In our relationship, Linda and I had already done a bit of travelling and hiking and carving out great little adventures near and far. I'd introduced her to boogie boarding and we'd had some great sessions at Lawrencetown and Conrad's Beach, and even on our travels to the UK. We were the only boogie boarders in the ocean most days, and those sessions took us into our own private little watery world of euphoria.

"If you feel up for it," I told her that first day as we crossed University Avenue and pulled into the hospital parking lot, "we'll go in the ocean after this is all over today."

"Are you crazy?" she asked.

"Most definitely," I answered. And I noticed that she was smiling.

The smile didn't last long. We parked and walked through what had become, for us, very ominous doors. We went up to the fifth floor in the Dickson Building, checked in at the desk, and waited until we were summoned to a treatment room, where Linda settled into what looked like a dentist's chair. There were several other people of various ages in the room, all getting chemo treatments. Some folks looked very sick; some may have been near death. There was one young woman who looked sad and pale. She wore a scarf over her bare head. The room was quiet except for the sound of ventilation system.

There was nothing cheerful about that place, and I doubt anything—not a fresh coat of paint nor a change of lighting nor the addition of new decorations—could change the feel of it. It felt like a place where people go to die.

The nurses were all of the highest calibre anyone could hope for. I sat beside Linda as the needle was inserted into her port and the IV bag positioned on the stand to drip the poison, which would hopefully kill the cancer cells, into her bloodstream. Sometimes we had to sit there and do nothing but wait for the pharmacy to send up the meds. Waiting is what you do in hospitals. It's a skill, we would learn. You could not rush things. You could not demand. You learned to wait patiently.

We were in the hospital for over six hours, which would become our usual day. My job was to keep Linda entertained, distracted, on track with feeling good about what we were doing. *Think of it like a job*, I said to myself more than once. *This is probably one of the most important jobs you'll ever have. Do it well.* Doing it well meant mostly learning to be patient and to let the nurses and doctors do what needed to be done.

I don't have much in the way of cheery little stories about the time we spent in those treatment rooms. I doubt whether anyone does. The patient gets drowsy from the drugs. A volunteer comes around with a little cart offering up free Pepsi, chicken salad sandwiches, and cookies. The nurses check to see if the drip is going well. Linda and I chat or read and look around. At noon, I go down to the cafeteria and buy a made-to-order large (and I do mean generously large) salad for us to split. (When a salad becomes the highlight of your day, you know you are in pretty desperate straits. But it was all part of the job.)

At the end of this particular hospital day, Linda looked and acted much sicker than she had when we had arrived that morning. I wondered if this was how it would always go. Would each successive toxic-but-necessary treatment knock her down more than the last? I helped her to the car and we drove home. Linda looked weary and diminished.

We didn't go boogie boarding after that first treatment. I think we were both mentally and physically exhausted. I thought perhaps I was deluding myself and Linda. Maybe this would *not* go well after all.

But by the second visit, we knew what to expect. The wait, the drip, the salad, the weary patient at the end of the day. But this time something was different. As we left the hospital and walked out into the bright sunshine, something changed. The wind was from the south, and even in the heart of Halifax we could smell the sea. "I want to go in the ocean," Linda said.

"Are you sure?" I asked. She didn't exactly look like a person ready to climb into a wetsuit and dive into a frigid ocean.

"You promised me," she said. "I want to go boogie boarding more than anything."

I thought she might change her mind by the time we made it out of the city and back to Lawrencetown. Instead, she grew more animated, more alive and more certain.

The sun was still bright when we hit the beach. The sea had that electric, pungent, fully-alive smell it sometimes has. We took great care getting Linda into her wetsuit, PowerPort notwithstanding. We grabbed our boards and walked out into the frothy waves. We caught our first waves of the day with the thrill of the drop, the arc of the wall of the wave, the locomotive thrust of the white water. Before long, we had tapped into all the positive energy and curative powers the sea had to offer.

I doubt anyone has ever said that boogie boarding is a cure for cancer. But I can assure you it is definitely good for the soul.

THE ROAD NOT TAKEN

I THINK I WAS IN GRADE SEVEN WHEN A GUIDANCE COUNSELLOR dutifully arrived in our classroom to give us a questionnaire that was supposed to help each of us determine which profession we should aim for when we grew up. In those days it seemed like we were being tested for everything. IQ tests were big and I did well on them, only to learn later that they were culturally biased (in my favour, as it turned out) and probably hogwash.

A week after taking the vocation quiz, I met with the guidance counsellor as he looked over my results, which had been interpreted by the folks who had conjured up the racket to bleed money from school boards across North America. The guidance counsellor was Mr. Naugler, who was locally famous for opening up the first public outdoor trampoline park in town (it was eventually shut down due to lawsuits).

Mr. Naugler told me the results indicated that I was not particularly good with people, and possibly not fond of people at all. He suggested I should find some sort of job that didn't require a lot of social interaction. I nodded and said that was okay by me. He said that, according to the findings, I would be good (and most happy) as a coal miner. Somehow the test had determined

I had an affinity for rocks. I'd been collecting various rocks and minerals since I was little, but I had never once thought of growing up to become a coal miner. Nonetheless, there it was, in black and white.

If coal mining didn't work out for me—possibly because I wasn't able to get along with the other miners—I should seriously explore heavy equipment operation. That sounded more like it! I could operate an earth-mover of some sort with massive tires.

The trouble was that, in those days, I really wanted to be a nuclear scientist. I'd read pamphlets about the wondrous new age of atom-splitting and nuclear reactors and wanted to be part of such an exciting field. I wrote enthusiastic biographical essays for my English teacher about famous nuclear scientists who had helped develop thermonuclear bombs and such. The phrase going around at the time was "Atoms for Peace," a phrase apparently conjured up by one of my father's war heroes, Dwight D. Eisenhower.

Coal mining, earth-moving, and splitting atoms all became "roads not taken" in my life. As you probably know, I've borrowed that phrase from the famous poem by Robert Frost in which "two roads diverged in a yellow wood." The poet has to decide on which road to take and he chooses the one "less travelled by," although a close study of the poem suggests that both paths are worn "about the same." Ever since this poem has come into the canon of school literature, it has probably been misinterpreted over and over again. The options for Frost were two overgrown, rarely hiked paths. He never even considered a well-travelled path: the one where you sell your soul in order to make a lot of money, I suppose. But perhaps that path was not an option there in the New England forest.

But, of course, the image and idea of the fork in the road representing life is most prescient. Once you make the decision and set on your path, paved with riches or smothered in leaf mulch, you probably will never go back and try the other route.

I've read way too much about alternate universes for my own well-being, but there are well-thumbed theories out there that the universe contains infinite versions of you…and, of course, me. So somewhere out there on another plane of existence is a version of me working in a coal mine, or me driving an earthmover. So be it.

Albus Dumbledore, in J. K. Rowling's *Harry Potter and the Chamber of Secrets*, says, "It is our choices, Harry, that show what we truly are, far more than our abilities." It is, indeed. Nuclear science faded by the time I was out of high school and I was sure I was destined to be a marine biologist—until I discovered that I was quite poor at chemistry, math, and even biology. Funny how that goes.

It turned out I was better at working with people than Mr. Naugler's test had predicted, and I was a whiz at writing, so I figured I could cobble together some kind of a mixed career of writing and teaching—which I did.

I was offered a teaching fellowship in Pocatello, Idaho, after graduating from university, and it seemed like a great opportunity until I discovered Pocatello was right next door to a nuclear testing range. I turned it down and went to graduate school in New York City until I felt the North calling to my soul and made the decision to move to Nova Scotia.

As I was settling in here in the early 1980s, oil prices were skyrocketing and there was considerable interest in renewable energy. We called it "alternative energy" in those days, and I got a job documenting backyard inventors in Atlantic Canada who were working with solar, wind, and tidal energy. A few years later, the federal government foolishly pulled the plug on most funding for research or implementation of such alternatives, and we went back to being an oil economy. If only we had stayed on that road not taken, we would have become one of the most energy-advanced nations in the world. But it was not to be.

With unemployment came my first encounter with Unemployment Insurance—UI, as it was known back then. Meeting with a government employment counsellor, I was again confronted with vocational options. I told the interviewer that my profession was that of an "alternate energy consultant," because that was what I had been doing. She politely told me there was no category on her computer for such a trade and asked me to look over the list of "real" jobs. It was a hefty list that, of course, included coal miner and heavy equipment operator. But, clearly, I did not have those skills. However, "poet" was listed as a legitimate occupation by the computer program. Having recently published my first book, I asked her to tick that one off, and she kindly did.

"Has your office received any recent requests for a poet?" I asked.

"No," she said. "But we will call you if we do."

As required, I made myself available for work—anything that might come up for a newly minted Canadian poet. Turns out there just wasn't much in the way of occupational opportunities for a poet in those days, so my time on UI allowed me to write and to explore teaching possibilities.

When it comes to job decisions, or any other important life decision for that matter, how do we know if we are making the right one? Maybe we don't. Some people make lists of the pros and cons; I've done that, and it is useful. Other people follow their gut. That works for some, but not for everyone.

But I know a couple of things about the endless diverging paths: first, whichever path you choose will probably turn out to be nothing like what you expected. You may even find that the path becomes completely overgrown and you end up lost in the woods—which may be just what you need. Or maybe it will turn out that you are already lost in the woods and you have to create your own path—create your own job.

Making life decisions can be quite scary. Whatever your decision is, I advise that you make sure it's yours and not someone else's. Coal mining and earth-moving can be, I am sure, noble, (albeit difficult) occupations, but they were clearly not for me.

So, if you are trying decide on an occupation, do this: envision yourself waking up on a Monday morning at some point a week, a month, or ten years in the future. How do you feel on that morning about the day ahead? If you are waking up to a job that is just that—a job—think again. If you are feeling that it would be exciting to get to work that morning, you may have nailed down your calling.

THE DEATH OF A FATHER

M Y FATHER, GEORGE CHOYCE JR., KNOWN TO MANY AS SONNY, passed away early in the morning on December 3, 2014. I had arrived home the afternoon before that to find him holding his great-grandson, Cooper, who was just a few months old. My ninety-three-year-old dad looked happy and content and, although he was having some breathing problems if he exerted himself, seemed to be more or less in good shape. Even though he was a bit tired, he was most certainly in good spirits.

I had been down this road several times before—flying to Philadelphia from Nova Scotia, thinking this might be the last time I saw my father alive. That same drama had played out a number of times with my mom, Norma Willis Choyce, who had declined slowly but steadily over her final years from a form of dementia. During that time, my dad had watched over and taken care of her, and had always, always, worried more about her than himself.

She had died in late November 2013 with her family by her side in the living room of their house. She had waited for me to arrive, I am sure; she took her last breath only minutes after I had kissed her forehead.

And so here I was, a year later, visiting my father and wondering if it was near the end. The two of us sat in the same living room, reminiscing and occasionally watching TV. Here was a man of ninety-three who was fully alert. Although he had been knocked down from his former physical self by a lingering cancer, he was most certainly living his life. He may have been waiting for his time to die, but he intended to live—really live—until that moment caught up with him.

So it was a kind of funny scene that evening; he liked to watch RFD-TV, which was a channel dedicated to farmers and farming issues. On my previous visit we had watched a half-hour show, produced by the Tennessee Department of Agriculture, about how to deal with farming problems caused by a growing wild boar population in the southern US. Had anyone stopped my dad and me on the street and asked us how to deal with their wild boar problem, we could have instructed them on how to build a pen made of chain-link fence, how to lure wild boar in at night while watching from a hidden camera using infrared technology, and how to close the pen by remote control from the comfort of their farmhouse kitchen.

On this night, the shows concerned how to get higher crop yields of corn and soybeans, and why any farmer with half a brain should be growing sorghum as a rotation crop. While Midwestern farmers spoke highly of the new breeds of corn, my dad was thumbing through a carton of pay stubs from 1957. "Sixty-seven dollars a week before taxes," he said, holding one up to show me. He had been working at a large New Jersey dairy company called Millside Farms in those days, servicing those milk trucks that drivers drove standing up as they delivered glass bottles of fresh milk to doorsteps around South Jersey. I would have been six years old in 1957 and we would have recently moved into a new house—one he and my mother built, cinder block by cinder block, board by board. This was the house we were sitting in at that moment—the one where they had lived most of their adult lives, my mother and father, and the house where they would both die—as was their desire.

Toward the end of his life, my father never hesitated to make it clear that he had had enough of hospitals and wasn't going back to one, no matter what. These days, when anyone came into the house, he showed them the notice he had put on the fridge. "Do No Resuscitate," it read ominously, but he would always smile when he pointed it out. Not that it was a joke—it was just the way things should be.

After a bit, we got talking, so we gave up on a crash course in sorghum fertilizers and I picked up an old photo album from a nearby table. I had not seen this one before. The photos were from 1942 and my father looked impossibly young. He had a "new" car—an old Plymouth, I think. In the photo, he leaned against the car and smiled at the camera—so youthful and cocky and, I suppose, preparing to go off to war. But this was one happy young dude.

He pointed out people in the photos I could not recognize, and he knew every name and detail about who they were. Page after page of smiling young men and women of the 1940s gazed out at me: brothers and sisters, aunts and uncles, friends, and my father's own parents. There were photos of a young Norma Willis, the beautiful woman who would be his wife. It was a black-and-white world, but it was not short on glamour and optimism, and it was a place where a young couple could start a family and build a home. We looked at some other photos from the early 1950s when they had started building the house. He reminded me that he had begun to dig the basement one shovelful at a time, sometimes with the help of a brother or two kind enough to assist with the task, until they discovered a bulldozer could do the whole job in about an hour.

He told me some stories that evening—some new, some familiar, all with the happy inflection of a man who had lived a good life, a happy life—a man who had no regrets and was at peace with the world.

Somewhere around 2:30 in the morning I woke to the sound of my brother Gordy's voice in the living room where my father lay in his borrowed hospital bed. I got up to see if I could help; Gordy had helped Dad sit upright in a chair as he had requested. Margaret, Gordy's wife, came in as well. Within minutes, Dad said there was a pain in his chest, and that he just wanted to be held. While Gordy gave our dad a small dose of prescribed morphine under his tongue, I held my father for a few short minutes, until his body relaxed and he slumped forward in my arms.

It's a tough thing to watch a father die, but his sons were there with him. He was in his own home, and he was most certainly looking forward to his reunion with his wife. In so many respects, a death doesn't get much better than that.

Some would have considered Sonny a fairly simple man. He was most certainly humble, modest, and unpretentious. He had not finished high school because he'd needed to go to work in the farm fields to help feed the large family he grew up in. He had gone to war, but never fired a shot. Instead, he'd driven military trucks without headlights down the dark, narrow roads near Cambridge, England, and hauled airplane parts from Land's

End, where a bomber had crash-landed. He'd returned home after the war, married, had two kids, and gone to work. He became a truck mechanic, often going off to work before dawn to get a fleet of diesel trucks on the road. He did road calls and changed truck tires on the Jersey Turnpike in the middle of snowstorms. He worked long and he worked hard.

Sonny was a farmer at heart and, in his teenage years, had done every dirty job imaginable on a farm, including dousing cabbages with insecticide—pure arsenic—all day long, until he returned home at night, covered head-to-toe in that pure white poison. After he'd built that legendary home, he'd always had a garden in front of the house in a triangular piece of land at the intersection of Church and Lenola Roads in Cinnaminson, New Jersey. He grew the best corn, peppers, green beans, lima beans, onions, eggplant, and squash any man could. And the tomatoes! He grew tomatoes the size of softballs that tasted better than any store-bought tomato ever had.

When he retired, he worked his garden, he grew Christmas trees, he tore down old buildings for wood to build a garage, and he collected scrap metal to haul to the junkyard for spare change. All of this was his idea of a good time.

But the sum total of the man was far more than the basic parts. My father's legacy was his sense of giving. More than anyone I can think of, he was selfless man. He helped others, he did good, and he did not do so out of a sense of duty, but because he wanted to. In his sixties, he helped look after some older friends who were in their eighties. In his seventies, he helped look after other friends who were in their nineties. By the time he hit his mid-eighties, there just weren't any folks much older than him around that he could help out.

He had grown up in poverty and yet he claimed he had not felt much deprived of anything. As a result, he rejoiced in his good fortune at having a home, a wife, a job, sometimes some chickens to raise for eggs, and a well-appointed garden.

He showed compassion for others and, even though there were a lot of things about the more modern world he did not understand, I believe he appreciated people who were different from him. He had an innate tolerance of his fellow men and women. In his own way, he lived large and he lived well.

Gordy and I were supremely privileged to have been raised by two such fine parents. More than ever, I can now appreciate that I get to go about my daily life as an adult without any real emotional scarring or baggage from my youth. Sonny and Norma gave my brother and me a good start, particularly when it came to homemade meals. We always had homemade sandwiches—liverwurst (my favourite), ham, and homegrown tomatoes, or meatloaf. Yep, even as recently as the year 2000 my mom was packing me one-and-a-half meatloaf sandwiches, made with homemade relish, for the flight back to Nova Scotia.

When I was a kid, our meals had almost always included food grown by my father and preserved by my mother: stewed tomatoes (not my favourite), but also frozen corn, lima beans, potatoes grown by my grandfather, and homemade tomato juice that included four kinds of vegetables and was so thick you could float a quarter on it.

It seemed odd that, as my mom was fading and after she was gone, my dad ate mostly prepared food from plastic containers or fast food purchased by Gordy from McDonald's or Wendy's. But at that point it was, for him, a matter of keeping things simple. He seemed to approve of any dish that involved ground beef, but he was also a fan of a good breakfast—especially a Spanish omelette on a Sunday morning at the Penn Queen Diner in Pennsauken, New Jersey.

Of course, there is much, much more to his life than that, and the details would come back to me in the weeks and months ahead through small images and fragments of memory.

It's safe to say my dad was always there for me. He accepted his son as a hitchhiking hippie, an overly opinionated young man, and a restless soul in his late twenties who believed he needed to leave the US for a new life in Nova Scotia. He always treated me fairly and was never harsh to judge. I knew he was always my dad and my source of strength.

Sonny loved people and he loved to talk. I doubt many would call him a philosopher, but I would. He taught me patience and persistence and compassion and optimism. He taught me to be fair and understanding. He taught me not to expect too much from the world, but to work hard and accept whatever small rewards the world gave back with humility and gratitude.

It's a bit of a cliché, but his passing is truly the end of an era. You won't see another Sonny Choyce in this new century.

Not long after he died, I found myself fixing a flat tire on a rental car by the side of the road in a small town in Italy. Linda and I had pulled off near the wall of an imposing granite church. I discovered I didn't have all the tools I needed, so I walked back to the cottage we had rented and brought back a knife to pry off the plastic wheel cap. On the way back to the car, I picked up a brick. If there was one thing my dad had taught me, it was to always block one of the wheels of a car when you change a tire so the car wouldn't roll. I guess I felt he was there with me in Italy, changing that tire with a spindly jack on the sloping pavement.

That brick kept the car steady as we removed the lug nuts and mounted the spare.

And I guess that's the final thing I have to say about him: he was steady. He was reliable. He kept us safe. He was dependable and always there—in Italy or anywhere else—whenever I needed him.

THE CARE AND FEEDING OF THE SUBCONSCIOUS MIND

S OMETIMES, WHILE TEACHING MY UNIVERSITY CREATIVE WRITING class, I find myself lecturing about the so-called subconscious mind and its relationship to writing fiction, but also to solving everyday problems. This is one of those times when I drift off into musings about things I technically know very little about but feel compelled to share. I can usually tell from their facial expressions that some students find it fascinating while others think I'm just rambling.

My understanding of the subconscious mind, I admit, is the artsy-fartsy version and not the psychology-textbook one. I did take a few psychology courses back in university, but the only one I remember was Abnormal Psych, where the big message seemed to be that no one was normal. Nonetheless, I've convinced myself that, in my writing career, I've learned a thing or two about the workings of the human mind worth sharing.

The way I understand it, your subconscious is the part of your thinking that is non-rational, somewhat instinctive, highly imaginative, and ultimately (if used properly) creative. Your dreams, daydreams, fantasies, wildly irrational thoughts, inner voices, visions, and creative work all come from there. If you are a writer or an artist, you damn well better be good friends with your subconscious.

As noted, I haven't dissected Einstein's brain or studied MRI scans to come to my conclusions. I've just cultivated my subconscious so it will work for me in ways that are useful for writing novels, poetry, or—well, what you're reading here. In fact, I once woke up asking myself what I should write about next, and sure enough, as if on cue, my subconscious answered that I should write about *it*. So I did.

That's how it works. Really. It's that simple. You ask your subconscious a question and it gives you an answer. Not always on cue, but eventually and reliably.

Back in the 1970s, when I was still living in the US, I was standing on a noisy, crowded corner of 42nd Street in New York City when I asked my subconscious if I should move to Canada— to Nova Scotia, in particular. Above the din of the traffic, it most emphatically said I should. So I did.

And since that turned out well, I started trusting my subconscious. If I wanted to figure out a title for a book when I was stuck, or determine what plot line or real-life resolution to come up with, I'd pretend my subconscious was like a computer. I'd internally pose the problem to my subconscious, then I'd stop thinking about it with my conscious mind. Lo and behold, a title, a plot, or a solution to life's everyday quandaries would be delivered down the line. It might come quickly, or it might take a few days or even a week. But when I *wasn't* thinking about it, the answer would be delivered like a well-timed Purolator package. And nine times out of ten, it was a damn good answer.

The trick to using this irrational faculty is to file the problem and then go away. Don't keep chewing it over in your rational mind like a piece of gristle you just chomped into at the Steak and Stein. Just let the ol' subconscious do its trick.

I see you in the class rolling your eyes—you science majors and pre-law students. Perhaps I need to elaborate.

The subconscious is probably related to your "gut instinct," some really primitive part of you that alerts you to the presence of the metaphorical lion in the office or shopping mall. It tells you to turn and confront the beast, or to run the other way, or just to grovel on the floor and be done with it.

Your gut instinct may be left over from your ancestors, but you have probably cultivated it in this life. Your rational mind tells you one thing, but your gut tells you another. I'd suggest you should always follow your gut, but I've noticed many people have very poor instincts when it comes to important decisions. Some folks just make bad decisions over and over. These people should probably fix that before they start relying too heavily on anything in their irrational domain.

Gut instinct is a close cousin to intuition. One of my favourite intellectual outlaws, R. Buckminster Fuller, creator of the geodesic dome, has said, "What I call then the Intuition, is a twilight zone existing between the subconscious and the conscious." So it is clearly a powerful and important element of your irrational being—as is the conscience.

I've been asked if and how the subconscious is related to the conscience—that part of your mind that tells you what you *should* do, even when you don't want to do it. Well, the truth is your conscience isn't particularly creative, although your parents probably had your best intentions in mind when they hammered it into shape. In my case, it was my parents and Walt Disney, because I still think of my conscience as Jiminy Cricket (of *Pinocchio* fame) who always said: "Let your conscience be your guide." I admit it's disconcerting to think that many of the important moral decision in my life were based on instructions from a talking cricket, but there it is.

So for big life decisions (beyond the scope of artistic and creative projects) you should make handy use of gut instinct and conscience if both are functioning properly. But I'm hoping you'll give audience to the subconscious as well.

Many writers of novels, poetry, and creative nonfiction are asked where we get our ideas. The truth is, many of us just listen to the voices in our heads. (Yes, there are voices. Sometimes there are even visions.) In olden times, those who heard voices and had visions might have been considered oracles or visionaries, whereas today they may be thought to have schizophrenia. I'm sure there are some bad voices wanting to surface from the subconscious and they are best to be ignored. There's certainly a lot of unusual stuff stashed away up there in the attic. Just try to make sense of a dream after a late-night slice of pepperoni pizza.

My voices tend to be weird, but they're often pretty interesting, and some of them are quite grand. I leave the silly stuff in an appropriately black garbage bag by the side of my psychological curb on the proper day of the week. But I cultivate the good ideas. And these are not the voices of God or of aliens or demons. The news all comes from my well-nurtured subconscious.

Steve Martin suggests that the conscious mind is the editor and the subconscious is the writer. And of course, once your subconscious has delivered the package, you must reluctantly turn it over to your rational mind to make sense of what's inside. Writing is fun; rewriting is hard work. If you are not writing, but working at other tasks, the same rule still applies: create and then revise.

You may prefer to think of your subconscious mind as your imagination. I think of imagination as part of the deeper well of the subconscious. Maybe when you were a child you were accused of having "too much imagination" so you toned it down—you said goodbye to imaginary playmates; you stopped seeing ghosts and witches. And then you grew up and got a proper job and set your imagination aside as something childish and impractical. Maybe it is time to bring it back into play. And "play" is certainly the operative word for it.

Once I finished my Abnormal Psych class back at Rutgers in 1972, I mostly gave up trying to read Sigmund Freud, whose theories at that point were being abandoned like unwanted cargo on a sinking ship. But when he wasn't obsessing over sex or drugs, he did say a few wise things that still resonate today. Freud wrote: "The conscious mind may be compared to a fountain playing in the sun and falling back into the great subterranean pool of subconscious from which it comes." If you haven't jumped into the pool for a while, watch for an opportunity—and go for a swim. The water is really quite nice once you get used to it.

SOMETHING ABOUT A GOOD WALK

S OME TIME ROUGHLY SIX MILLION YEARS AGO, A FEW OF OUR dissatisfied ancestors thought it was getting a bit too hard on the knuckles to transport their carcasses on all fours, so these forward-thinking whiners decided to stand up straight and walk on two feet. They liked it a lot. Eventually this new fad caught on, and more and more early humans began ambulating upright; they found it gave them distinct advantages.

These far-distant ancestors of ours are now known as *Sahelanthropus tchadensis* and they lived in the grasslands of Central Africa. Perhaps we'll never know why they decided to stand upright and begin striding around, but it likely had much to do with survival. Running, no doubt, came about soon after walking and it was a great means to chase animals for food, or to prevent oneself from becoming food for other carnivorous wild beasts. Generally speaking, in those days, you only ran only when you had to. No one really went out for a morning jog.

Today, some of us still find walking gratifying and not a chore. We are a rather lazy, urban lot, and we sometimes forget about walking for fun and health. If we go out walking in a rural setting, we call it hiking. To a video game addict or a hockey-watching fanatic, it probably sounds boring, but a good hike can soothe the soul, enhance the circulation, and improve brain activity.

Okay. Sorry. I've been listening to too many self-improvement CDs while driving my car. I just meant to say that hiking (or mere walking) can sometimes fix what ails us if we give it a chance.

I personally like getting off the main trails and just walking in the woods. Along my hurricane-ravaged coast, that often means climbing and stumbling over fallen spruce trees and tripping over tangles of raspberry canes. Our coastal forests can be dense and jungle-like, with barriers of dense evergreen trees creating nearly impenetrable walls. It's not most people's idea of a pleasant hike, but I rather like the challenge.

Although it sounds foolish, I actually enjoy walking into a forest without trails and getting lost. I'm not advising this, lest I get angry letters from the search and rescue people. In truth, I don't get *really* lost. Just partially lost. I sometimes carry a compass and, after finding myself deep inside a chunk of forest wilderness, use it to get myself pointed in the right direction—back to civilization.

Not everyone knows what a compass is. A few years ago, while I was boarding a plane, a young security guard searched my backpack. She found my old Boy Scout compass and looked at me suspiciously. She showed it to another young security guard and he shrugged. They didn't know what it was, but they thought it might be dangerous. I was taken out of line and asked about the nature of this suspicious-looking device. I answered, "It's a compass."

"What does it do?" she asked. I tried to explain that it told me where north was, and that seemed to mystify her even more. She was about to get her supervisor when I explained that it helped me find my way to locations. "Oh," she said. "You mean like a GPS." She returned the ancient device to me and I flew off, according to my compass, due south.

I've occasionally found myself lost in Nova Scotian forests without a compass, and have prided myself on finding my way out by sniffing the air for salt and just heading toward the sea. I've cautiously tried other pathfinding tricks in other provinces with less success. I don't seem to do so well in those locations where there is no ocean nearby.

I met my ultimate match one day in early May in the Northwest Territories, when I went hiking in the wilderness outside Yellowknife on what was supposedly a relatively well-marked path. What I thought was a trail turned out to be a track used by Arctic hare and grouse, and I found myself sitting on a boulder with a raven laughing at me as I realized I was well and truly lost.

With no compass or sea wind to guide me, I decided that if I made a wrong decision, I'd be royally screwed, so I sat down and thought it through. The bad news was that if I picked a direction to walk in and it turned out to be a faulty guess, I might go hundreds, if not a thousand, kilometres before I would run into civilization.

So, cautiously, I began to walk in circles around my boulder, in wider and wider arcs, over and over, until I found an overgrown but tangible trail. Eventually I stumbled out of the wilderness with sore feet and a bruised ego. Thus did I realize my hobby of getting lost could be dangerous in the wrong patch of woods.

Nonetheless, I find that most coastal forests in Nova Scotia are great places to walk and get lost in, as long as there are no blackflies or mosquitoes. They can ruin a good walk in much the way a game of golf did for Mark Twain. "Golf is a good walk spoiled," said the author of *Adventures of Huckleberry Finn* (although he apparently wasn't the first to say it).

But I presume most hikers don't necessarily enjoy getting lost in the woods and clambering over fallen trees, slogging through boggy wilderness, or having saplings snap cruelly in their faces. Most prefer a well-groomed forest trail or a beach with hard-packed sand, or even the well-appointed Trans-Canada Trail that snakes through this fair province with its mostly flat track of class-A gravel.

Although I think of myself as a seasoned off-road rambler, I've been humbled again and again by more experienced hikers. Once, in the Cinque Terre region of Italy, Linda and I followed an ancient footpath that took us from the coastal community of Riomaggiore all the way to Manarola. The path along the sea had been washed out, so we took an alternate mountain path, a mere couple of kilometres long, according to my map. The ascent was brutally steep and my heart was pounding as we climbed the treacherous mountain trail. Italian men who looked like they were in their eighties or nineties overtook us handily as they headed up the slopes to tend their grapes. It made me realize what a wimp I was when it came to mountain hiking.

On another occasion, we were hiking up a mountain in the western corner of North Carolina, planning to join up with the Appalachian Trail. We had been doing a fair bit of hiking around the Great Smoky Mountains and I had strained my knee. Near the summit I admitted I was in serious pain, but we pushed on to the top for the most extraordinary view of Tennessee and North Carolina.

Much to my chagrin, when we began to descend I discovered that walking downhill hurt even more, and we were several kilometres from where we had parked the car. I limped along as best I could until we came to a gathering of hard-core hikers who were in the midst of traversing the entire Appalachian Trail from Georgia to Maine. We stopped to chat and they introduced themselves by their nicknames: Hobo Dave, Wild Willy, Mountaintop Milly and Leave-Me-Alone-Leon. Recognizing us as mere day-hikers, they subtly let us know we were rank amateurs: lowly mortals not to be taken seriously in the realm of multi-state hikers. I asked for advice about my bad knee and Hobo Dave offered me some sympathy and a couple of Tylenol.

I thanked him profusely and limped off toward the Tennessee River and our car, which was parked near the Fontana Dam. I wondered what it would be like to hike for months through the remaining great forest wilderness of the eastern seaboard. Although it would not be for me, I knew those hikers were modern pilgrims on a quest, looking for solace and inspiration in the woods, and I admired them greatly.

For those who don't like the idea of getting lost in the woods or trekking the length of a mountain range, there is still much to be said for simply walking. Something called "walk-and-talk therapy" is becoming popular in the US and elsewhere, and it appears to work very well. How does it work? Well, you walk. And, yes, you talk while you are walking. In New York City, of course, you pay two hundred dollars or more per hour for a therapist who specializes in this sort of thing. He or she takes you for a hike around Central Park or wherever, and you talk about your problems. According to WebMD, Toronto psychologist Kate Hays says this form of therapy "helps a patient get 'unstuck' when confronting difficult issues" and "spurs creative, deeper ways of thinking."

Hell, yes. Of course it does. But you don't need to pay a

shrink to do it. You don't even need a companion. If you prefer, you can walk (and talk) by yourself. As you walk forward, the walking psychologists say, you also tend to sway side to side. As you fall into a pattern, you discover that this motion feels quite nice. Your mind settles down. Your heart settles into a soothing rhythm as your breathing deepens and becomes more regular. This is partly due to the "bilateral coordination" going on. You are linking up both sides of your body and you are integrating the left and right hemispheres of your brain—or so the experts say.

And the end result is that your body and your mind are improved and enhanced.

And, of course, that is nothing new. What those ancient upright ancestors of ours in the grasslands of Africa did when they had a bad day, felt out of sorts, or truly experienced tragedy in their lives was quite simple: they probably went for a walk. The larger the tragedy, the longer the walk. So, if your life has got you down, toss the car keys and go for a walk—the longer, the better.

MURDO'S STORY

IN 2014, OUR TWELVE-YEAR-OLD DOG, MURDO, WAS DIAGNOSED with advanced bladder cancer. It's a sad truth that most of us outlive our dogs, and I've outlived several, so I wasn't looking forward to the heart-wrenching decline of another pet.

Despite the bad news, we weren't ready to give up on the old boy. We put him on some rather expensive medication, knowing it would not cure him but that it would ease any discomfort and extend his life. As far as I could tell, most of his days were good, as Linda and I did all we could to give him a prolonged life with quality care.

Don't get me wrong: if Murdo had been in pain or distress, we were prepared to do what needed to be done. But we would cherish the time we still had with him.

Murdo, a West Highland White Terrier (better known as a Westie), came into my life fully grown as part of a new relationship that blossomed into a marriage. I got a wife and a dog all in one package. If I recall correctly, the first time Murdo came into my home, he immediately marked his territory by peeing on a wall. The manoeuvre was effective, even if it was not intentional.

The name Murdo, as you might have guessed, is Scottish

in origin and it means "mariner" or "protector of the sea." Although Murdo was not overly fond of the ocean and was somewhat wary of the waves that sometimes caught him off guard, I noticed he liked to bark with great determination at seagulls. Perhaps he thought the swooping gulls were attacking the Atlantic, pelting it with their hazardous gull-droppings, and thus he was trying to ward them off in his assigned role as ocean protector.

Dogtime.com has this to say about the breed: "The best way to describe this wee white terrier breed of Scotland is simply to say that he's so full of self-esteem that he knows he's the best thing around." I can attest that the Dogtimers have done their research, and I have always liked dogs with high self-esteem.

The 16th Laird of Poltalloch is given credit for the development, early in the twentieth century, of the modern breed of Westie, although records of small white terriers go back to the time of James VI who had his way with England from 1567 to 1625. At one point during his reign he had twelve of the lively little beasts shipped to the king of France as a gift.

Legend suggests that Westies ended up being white because trigger-happy British huntsmen kept shooting the reddish or tan-coloured terriers, thinking they were foxes. The breed was, and still is, very good at chasing a variety of wild animals. In olden times, they were particularly good at chasing, catching, and presumably eating, rats. If you had watched Murdo lying in a pool of sunlight on the living room floor, you would have seen how he could "unhinge" his back legs as if he was ready to crawl through some rat's underground tunnel and fetch the offending rodent for his master.

Murdo and I became fast friends, and he accompanied me

many times on my trips to the beach to check the surf conditions, as well as on hikes up headlands and into the woods. Like any terrier worthy of his breed, he would occasionally knock over trash cans and eat garbage, run off into the underbrush after snowshoe hares, bite the ankle of the Purolator man, or get into a snarling fight on the beach with a dog four times his size. He was just that kind of dog. In his heyday, without a proper leash, he would run out into the road after a school bus or a garbage truck and attempt to bite the tires of the offending vehicle, which his primitive brain believed to be a hostile creature.

I had never heard of dog grooming until Murdo came into my life. Certainly, you would spray your mutt down with the garden hose after he'd rolled in something putrid, or you might occasionally reward him with an actual bath if it seemed like the thing to do (after which, of course, the dog would jump from the tub and enthusiastically shake, spraying the walls and furniture). But Westie grooming is, apparently, an art best left to professionals, and those professionals tend to charge accordingly. Thus, while my wallet was, on occasion, emptied of its contents, I am not bitter about the financial loss, and I might now even suggest it was money well spent...but probably not.

After the biopsy and the prognosis, Linda and I decided to hold off on a planned trip and stay home to be with Murdo, especially so we could be there when his time came. We cancelled reading tours and vacations, often after old Murdo had taken a somewhat slight turn for the worse, only to bounce back quite quickly once he had determined we were not going anywhere.

I don't mention this as a complaint, just an odd little bit about how dogs can rule our lives—as many of you well know.

During Murdo's final summer, we had a family of raccoons

marauding the property, digging into garbage bins, and climbing up to raid bird feeders. They're fun to watch as they scamper about, but we didn't want Murdo to tangle with the unpredictable masked mob, so we usually kept him tied up when he was outside. One rainy night, however, he bolted out the door and went dashing off into the thick jungle of spruce and fir just beyond the lawn. I heard him barking and then screeching and I was certain he was being attacked by the raccoons.

I had only recently read in the *Chronicle Herald* about a young woman in the province who'd had to save her own dog from a raccoon. The dog had chased after the creature and, in its own defense, the raccoon had gone into a lake and had lured the dog, who was at least three times its size, to follow. When the dog's owner came on the scene, the dog was mid-lake with the wily raccoon on its head, trying to drown it. The woman had to swim out to save her dog from the raccoon. Fortunately, she was successful.

It was pouring rain the evening Linda and I went smashing through the wet branches to get to what we were sure was an attempt by a raccoon family to kill poor, misguided Murdo. I ran deep into the woods and Linda arced around near the lake just in case. When Murdo stopped screeching, we were both sure we had failed in our rescue mission. We regrouped on the lawn, panting and fearful, only to see Murdo emerge from the woods a few minutes later. He was dirty and bleeding, but he was alive. He was a bit traumatized by the skirmish, but otherwise okay. And once he was back in the safety of our home, the adventure seemed to have improved his appetite.

I occasionally called Murdo "the million-dollar dog" because of the amount of money we spent on vet bills, anti-cancer drugs, and, of course, those monthly grooming sessions. As we continued to give him Piroxicam (an anti-inflammatory drug for arthritis) and Misoprostol (to treat stomach ulcers), we declined further surgery after a first effort that removed part of the offending tissue. There was some talk of taking him to Charlottetown for an operation that would remove his bladder and implant a tube to be attached to a urostomy bag, but we just didn't think that was going to be a good life for a dog. Still, I believed we should do more to help, so eventually I did what we all do these days when we want to learn how to do things like change the blade on our lawn mower, watch American Netflix, stop our feet from sweating, or determine what others have to say about ailments (human or otherwise): I went on the internet. I googled "alternative treatments for cancer in dogs" and discovered I had much to learn.

Soon, I stumbled on something called "The Jim Kelmun Protocol" and it sounded so fabulously laughable that I was determined to give it a try on ol' Murdy. You will probably think I made this up, but I did not. It called for heating up a mixture of one part baking soda and three parts maple syrup, and giving him one teaspoon a day. There was even "research" to back this up.

An author named Mark Sircus wrote about alkalinity and cancer in his self-published e-book, *Sodium Bicarbonate—Rich Man's Poor Man's Cancer Treatment*. Sometimes molasses is used instead of maple syrup, but, hey, this is Canada, so we are richly endowed with the right stuff for the job.

It seemed absurd, but somehow this treatment echoed in my brain as the real thing. My grandmother Minnie had religiously believed you could clean or cure just about anything with the right combination of baking soda and vinegar. So why not cancer? The theory behind the protocol is this: you give your pooch a teaspoon of the mixture and the cancer cells gobble up the sweet maple syrup, which is only a Trojan horse for the sodium bicarbonate—an alkaline that supposedly attacks and kills cancer cells.

Well, all I can tell you is that, along with his prescribed meds, Murdo got a regular dose of this "love potion" (as we called it) and, all things considered, he remained in relatively good health. You don't want to get me going too far on ideas about alternative therapy, but—what if? What if there are everyday cheap alternative and natural cures, not just for dog cancer, but for just about everything under the sun? Surely it would be bad news for multinational pharmaceutical companies, but otherwise much good could come of it.

Perhaps this is just wishful thinking. Murdo was not a big fan of the love potion. Historically, Westies probably haven't eaten a lot of baking soda or maple syrup, so I had to mask it with yet another Trojan horse—Cheez Whiz—to get it into his system. The things we do for the love of our pets, eh?

I was all too aware that somewhere down the line, Murdo would breathe his last breath. We had narcotics on hand and an emergency plan to ensure he would not suffer. I had no idea whether that day was near or distant but, like everyone who lives with a loved one afflicted with illness, I took it one day at a time.

So I leave you with one final story, which really isn't much of a story; more like an image. One night when Linda was having a hard time sleeping, she got out of bed and went into the living room to read a book about death and dying. At night, we tried to keep Murdo in a doggie bed on a large chair positioned by the side of our bed. Usually, however, he ended up with us, often wedged between us or gradually stretching out from side to side until one or the other of us was left sleeping on a narrow piece of bed real estate—much like, say, Chile in relation to Argentina.

However, on this particular night, I turned toward Linda to put my arm around her. Unfortunately for me, Murdo had planted himself facing the foot of the bed, with his butt resting comfortably on the pillow. Before I realized it, I had my head snuggled up against his hairy white backside. It was dark so I didn't fully realize what was going on, and when morning arrived, there was the dog—white as the beard of Santa Claus, his butt right in my face, and snoring in a most contented fashion.

Whether it was the veterinarian's drugs or the Kelmun Protocol or sheer good luck, Murdo lived much longer than expected. Finally, one cold February day, we realized something had changed for our beloved pet. Dogs often don't let you know if they are in pain, but this day was different. We called the vet and she kindly came to the house to do what needed to be done.

Murdo's time had come.

FEAR AND FLYING

FOR MANY PEOPLE, FEAR AND FLYING GO TOGETHER. THE FEAR often involves the very logical thought that a large metal machine filled with luggage and people could stop working properly at thirty thousand feet and plummet directly to the earth with you on board, resulting in a fiery crash that would end your life. Some people stop flying altogether because of this fear.

Although I don't consider myself a well-heeled world traveller, I have flown to many wonderful dots on the globe, ranging from Labrador to Vancouver Island, from South Africa to Iceland, from Switzerland to Japan. I almost never worry about the plane crashing. Like many people, I have a voice in my brain that suggests to me: "Well, here you are again. You've paid your money and you are in your seat, and if anything really does go wrong with this flight, there is not a damn thing that you can do about it. You might as well try to relax and enjoy the clouds."

I remember once flying somewhere and watching a movie about a plane crash during the flight. The movie, *Fearless*, with Jeff Bridges, was about a man who walked away from the disaster, and I enjoyed it immensely (although I think some folks did complain to the flight attendants because the captain apologized for the selection toward the end of the flight).

As I get older, I am often startled to see how young other people are—especially those in positions of authority and responsibility. You may have noticed this yourself when it comes to airline pilots. I'm of the opinion that people who fly jumbo jets should all look (and act) like "Sully" Sullenberger (who famously landed US Airways Flight 1549 on the Hudson River in New York City in January 2009). But that's not always the case. Some of today's pilots, especially for the charter airlines, look like they should be in grade eight or grade nine. They have shiny faces and over-sized captain's uniforms like they are playing at being pilots and couldn't possibly be the real thing. But I reckon if someone has hired these lads or lasses to fly multi-million–dollar aircraft, the kids must be reliable.

I have had a few fearful moments on flights, though. Once, on a cheap flight from England to New York, a man refused to put his briefcase under the seat as we were landing, and he clutched it to his chest like a bomb. The flight attendant tried to pry it from him, and there was a scuffle as we descended to John F. Kennedy International Airport in the middle of a thunderstorm.

We landed and were boarded by New York city police officers wearing bulletproof vests, and the man was carted off. My guess is it was all just a misunderstanding. I was left, however, with a bad vibe about the plane itself—mostly because it seemed old and not well cared for. The company was called Arrow Air and one of their planes (it could have been the one I had been on) crashed in Newfoundland not long after that.

But that didn't stop me from flying. As often as I can muster, I try to remain a naive optimist, and the pose usually serves me well.

Of course, I've had those bumpy flights you see in all the

good plane-crash movies. Once, other passengers and I hastily loaded onto a small commercial plane for a short flight from Blanc-Sablon, Quebec, to St. Anthony, Newfoundland, because the pilot saw a brief break in a snowstorm that had been fore-casted to last for three days. It was a wild ride, and I should have feared for my life. The woman across from me was crying, and I offered her chewing gum and soothing words as the seat belt bit into my gut and my head banged against the back of the seat. The fear I saw in her eyes was as real as it gets.

And then there was this: I was flying home from Florida with my twelve-year-old daughter, Pamela, many years ago. We had gone to Walt Disney World in Florida (which is a wonderful vaca-tion for anyone who cherishes standing in long lines in the hot sun for hours at a time listening to complaining American children). A tornado had swept through Kissimmee, Florida, while we'd slept at the Holiday Inn the night before—after I had assured Pamela that there were no tornados in Florida. (Where do kids get such ideas?)

Oddly enough, as we loaded ourselves onto the plane to return to the relative safety of Canada, a dark cloud was forming in the direction toward which we were about to take off.

The captain (sounding like a very cocky young guy) informed us over the PA that indeed there was another tornado forming ahead, and we should buckle up quickly and get off the ground. He was confident we could get above it before it could do much harm.

My daughter was asking me a rapid string of nervous ques-tions and, before I could quiet her, a frantic-looking airline atten-dant leaned over and told her in no uncertain terms to "shut the hell up." That's when I knew things were serious.

But aside from some strong winds and a truly ominous-looking sky, we sailed away from Florida unscathed.

So, yes, flying does instill various forms of fear in all of us—me included. Almost every time I am about to fly, an irrational fear wells up in me as I drive to the airport. The fear is simply this: something could happen on this trip that means I never come back home. I'm not afraid of dying, exactly. I'm just afraid that I won't get to return to the life I love—my normal, everyday Nova Scotian life.

This fear feels like an omen or a warning (from God? from angels?) and it seems very real. But I override it. I push past it. Yet it's a good reminder of the fear other people might be experiencing and I decide again to be as kind and compassionate as I can to everyone I encounter while waiting to board the plane or while flying.

Airline travel can be a very stressful thing. Each of us feels the stress in some form or other, so we need to be kind to fellow travellers and airline people—we really do. All manner of things complicate travel: seating issues, overbooked planes, lost luggage, harried counter staff, ranters and ravers. The list, as you know, is endless.

The worst part of air travel for me is quite irrational: I just don't like being stuck in a seat for hours at a time. I wish there was enough room to get up and walk around. Although it's rare, I have sometimes felt trapped, anxious, and panicky, but it was never the plane itself that made me feel that way; it was me. At those times, I've envisioned a beautiful summer morning at Lawrencetown Beach and a glassy shoulder-high wave, and the wave has saved me every time.

Knowing how air travel can bring out fears and anxiety, I try to make it a point to be helpful to anyone who appears confused, fearful, nervous, or sad. Quite a few years back, I was trying to get home to Nova Scotia from Paris. I was coming down with a god-awful flu. I had taken the wrong train to the airport and had arrived a little late for my Air France flight to Montreal. I was stuck in a long line and was not allowed to move ahead. When I reached the counter, the Air France agent told me my seat had already been resold; I'd missed the two-hour advance deadline. The guy was nasty and rude, and he told me I had to go elsewhere to find another flight.

I sat in the airport with a fever for four hours, and then finally got on an Air Canada flight. When I arrived in Montreal, a snow-storm was raging and flights to Halifax had been cancelled. I don't think I'd ever felt so ill in my life. An older Air Canada agent saw my plight and offered a few kind words. She gave me a voucher for a nearby hotel and a slip for a free cab ride, but it was the way she treated me—with kindness—that made all the difference.

The stress potential for air travel today has been amped up exponentially from what it was in decades gone by. Sometimes, if you think about all the things that can go wrong, you just want to stay home, put your feet up on the coffee table, and watch reruns of *Mad Men*.

But there are places to see and people to meet, and all that stress is a good test of character. My plan is a simple one: the next time I fly, I intend to tuck my anxiety into my back pocket and sit on it. Then I'm going to think about how many times in my life I've relied for help on the kindness of strangers. And whenever the opportunity arises, I will attempt to be one of those strangers—someone who does the simplest little thing to help someone else when the going gets rough.

BEYOND TRANSCENDENTAL WOOD-SPLITTING

Recently I came across a quirky little article of mine that had been published in the *Globe and Mail* back in 1988 on the subject of splitting wood. Apparently, I was quite excited about it back in those days. Mornings would find me in an unheated room in a two-hundred-year-old farmhouse that had next to no plumbing, writing my second novel on an old 1960s Smith Corona manual typewriter that I had retrieved from someone's trash. Afternoons, when the surf was not good, I would be poised at the chopping block on the hillside, whacking a large axe into a big block of maple, oak, or beech. It didn't get much better than that.

In the article, I wrote about a phenomenon that sometimes occurred on very cold days when I was splitting wood. I referred to it as "transcendental wood-splitting." I was most intrigued by just about anything I thought was potentially "transcendental" in those days, and I had discovered that if you looked hard enough at most things in the known (or unknown) universe, virtually anything could be transcendental. Including wood-splitting.

It went like this: on certain bitterly cold days as I was putting logs upright on the chopping block and splitting each one from top to bottom, over and over, there seemed to be a split second—as the axe blade was falling, about to hit its mark—when I would suddenly hear a sound much like a rifle shot. The log would then split wide open, even before my axe blade connected with the wood. The head of the axe, with all my energy behind it, would then slice through empty air where the firewood had been and drive itself deep into the chopping block. If I was not prepared, the force could almost flip me over into the woodpile. I wondered how such a thing could happen, or if indeed it was quite simply a product of my overly fertile (and ever-enlarging) imagination.

It didn't happen all the time, mind you; only on rare occasions and only when it was very cold and I was splitting wood with a perfectly straight grain. There were attempts to document the event with a video camera but, like so many fleeting transcendental events in our lives, the magic shuts down once someone attempts to record it.

I had a theory, of course. I deduced that the wood was wet and that the water molecules had crystalized along the straight lines of the grain. I guessed that I had set up some kind of force field as I whacked on the upright logs over and over, so eventually the potency of the plummeting axe blade was producing enough energy, directed along those crystalline lines, to actually cleave the wood in half.

I'm sure the editors of the op-ed page at the *Globe* thought my little article was tongue-in-cheek, and they ran it, not for the edification of the Canadian public, but in the hope that it might bring a smile or a chuckle to someone commuting to downtown Toronto from Etobicoke.

After the piece ran, using the small sum paid to me for my words, I bought some more (not-split) firewood from a neighbour and continued to bang out on my typewriter what I thought would be a bestselling eco-thriller about evil corporate forces building a nuclear reactor on the unstable Karst topography of the south shore of Nova Scotia. As I recall, the climactic scene somewhere near the end involved hang-gliding, and I am sure there were good reasons why my protagonist had needed a hang glider to help save Nova Scotia from an imminent Chernobyl-like meltdown.

As the warmer weather had arrived, I'd been splitting less wood and had mostly forgotten all about metaphysical wood-splitting activities. But then the mail (what we now call "snail mail") began to arrive about the wood-splitting article. The newspaper had forwarded a few postcards and some envelopes that even included photographs—nothing terribly interesting or racy, just bearded men in heavy winter coats, splitting firewood. I can't say there was a flood of mail—more like a trickle. But there were others like me out there: men (and a few women) who had experienced the splitting of the wood before the blade had made its mark.

I was not alone in the transcendental wood-splitting universe. My brothers and sisters of the axe agreed that cold temperatures were a significant part of it. The postmarks suggested Labrador, Northern Ontario, Alberta, and the Yukon were prime areas for the phenomenon. All agreed that really "clean" wood was necessary—no knots or wavy grains, and certainly no softwood. Really dry wood was not quite right; logs frozen with ice in their veins were optimal (necessary for the force field to connect with the crystalline structure, of course!).

This was all very exciting to me. I like to think that, because of my article, I was dubbed "The Father of Transcendental Wood-Splitting," but in moments of sober reflection, I realize I may have made up that moniker myself.

Steven Spielberg's blockbuster movie *Close Encounters of the Third Kind* had come out a decade earlier and had made quite an impression on some of us. Now I began to wonder if those of us experiencing our out-of-the-ordinary moments at the chopping block were possibly select individuals who were receiving important (albeit somewhat quirky) messages about the nature of the universe. Had we been selected by super-intelligent aliens to gather together for some purpose—perhaps to save the world, our world, from ourselves?

After careful consideration, I came to the conclusion that it was unlikely that highly evolved sentient beings from distant galaxies would choose wood-splitting as the appropriate means to communicate with us from light years away. But then, maybe they thought they were communicating with our ancestors, not the modern humans we had become, or that only those of us still "primitive" enough to be splitting firewood for heat should have the privilege of getting to know them. When I tried either theory on my friends, they all suggested I had probably spent too much time alone in an unheated room writing fiction, and that I should get out more often.

I went back to thinking of other possible explanations. I recalled from my introductory university philosophy course that many philosophers had pondered things they considered "transcendent." When they weren't making arguments about what was real and what was not real, those wise and curious men sometimes explored the perimeters of our reality. Immanuel Kant, the eighteenth-century German philosopher, referred to judgments that pretend to have knowledge beyond the traditional boundaries on knowledge as "transcendent judgments." My ice-force-field explanation was perhaps too mundane, then, to be considered transcendental. But Kant was the one who eventually determined that the world "in itself" was unknowable.

Such thinking led me to ultimately reject my scientific (well, pseudo-scientific) explanation, and I decided what I had been doing on those rare-but-luminous moments when the crack had sounded and the axe blade had buried itself into the chopping block was this: I was splitting the wood with my mind.

Sadly, the more I pondered the whole thing, the less the magical event seemed to happen as I went about preparing firewood. It might just have been because the days grew warmer as we headed into spring, but I'm not sure it was just that. I should never have tried to film it or write about it; I should not have tried to think too hard about what it all meant.

In essence, I had questioned too much, looked too hard for the cause—and ultimately defiled the purity of a supernatural phenomenon. Some have argued that, many generations ago, before we developed our intellect, we were much more cognizant of and sensitive to natural and spiritual events around us. I believe that to be true. Our ancestors believed in miracles, inexplicable phenomena, and supernatural intervention of all sorts.

I feel privileged to have had my peep into the unknown, my brush with elemental realities usually beyond a mortal's grasp. I'm sad to say that now, nearly thirty years since my glory days of transcendental wood-splitting, I no longer split wood, and I no longer experience this extraordinary event. But I like to think I learned my lesson well.

PLACE NAMES OF NOVA SCOTIA, A–Z

O N MY DESK SITS A WELL-THUMBED BOOK PUBLISHED BY THE Canadian Board on Geographical Names. *Place Names of Nova Scotia, A–Z* is a gazetteer of Nova Scotia place names. It includes rivers, bays, islands, lakes, towns, capes, harbours, shoals, coves, brooks, banks, heads, spits, channels, hills, meadows, and more. Anything that has a name in the province (as of 1961) is listed therein, with its location. I'm fairly certain that a lot of these names have fallen out of common usage, but the book fascinates me because I've always found names of places intriguing, especially those that conjure up an unusual image.

I convinced my sculptor friend, Luigi Costanzo, to hike with me once to a place called Lake No Good. I'd discovered the name on a topographic map and it was just too tempting to pass up. On a muggy summer day we trudged up a little brook for several kilometres through dense spruce trees and overgrowth, only to discover it was a most ordinary lake. The mosquitoes and blackflies appreciated our efforts, however, and feasted upon our flesh. In the end, we agreed the lake had a fitting name. It's just north of the top end of Porters Lake, if you care to go there—but be sure to carry a good topo map and a big can of bug spray.

My other minor explorations to remote locations with interesting names produced much better results, so I'd like to share some of what I know of place names in Nova Scotia with a short tour through the gazetteer. Most of these places I've never been to, but exploring them on paper gives a varied lexical picture of our ever-enchanting province. Most are lesser-known places, so perhaps some will whet your appetite for adventure and you might want to seek them out. I'll just point out the highlights alphabetically. Rest assured there are hundreds, if not thousands, more place names all around us, some as mundane as Back Road (in Seaforth and elsewhere) and some as exotic as Garden of Eden (near New Glasgow).

But let's start with A.

Southwest of Shubenacadie, for example, is A Lake. Yep. Just the letter A. Sadly there is no B or C Lake. There is also an Amethyst Cove—most exotic, but hard to get to, and you may not want to trust those jury-rigged fraying ropes on the way down. Ankle Jack Lake near Bridgewater sounds like it might have a few stories—and I bet the fishing is good.

I always liked the sound of Baccaro Point on the south shore. If you're a fisher, you've heard it mentioned in the marine weather forecast a thousand times. There's a Bad Falls waiting for you in Yarmouth County, but you'd have to head toward Chester to find Bad Lake. There is also a Bad Luck Falls and, out at sea somewhere past Sober Island on the Eastern Shore, is the most curious Bad Neighbour Shoal.

The gazetteer suggests many of our Nova Scotian ancestors were not particularly creative (possibly even downright lazy) when they were coming up with a multitude of place names. Thus there are ten Bear Brooks listed, eight Bear Coves, seven Bear Islands, and well over twenty Bear Lakes. Clearly there used to be more bears in the province than there are now. You don't even want to ask about how many Beaver Creeks, Harbours, Islands, Lakes, and Ponds there are.

Pick a colour and you also have dozens of place names. "Black" appears often for rivers, points, and ponds, and the gazetteer lists at least a dozen Black Duck Lakes. If you're looking for a way to go back in time or to slip off to another part of the universe, I suggest either Black Hole Brook, flowing into Scots Bay, or the lovely Blackhole Meadow near Shubenacadie.

There must be stories behind each and every name, but most of those stories seem to have been lost over the years. And exactly who were those folks who first gave a place a name? Did someone once see a cabbage floating in Cabbage Garden Cove? The Camerons and the Campbells seem to have travelled far and wide in Nova Scotia naming things after themselves. And does anyone know if the so-called Chicken Rocks still exist in Bedford Basin, or have they been filled in and paved over for a Starbucks? I counted forty-two Cranberry Lakes but only two Cranberry Bogs, which is where I think you'd usually find the cranberries.

The Ds begin with Daddy Lake—very cool. A birthday present from the kids, maybe? *Hey, Dad, we named a lake after you.* Devils Island, of course, is in Halifax Harbour, but The Devils Burrow is a marshland north of Windsor (probably a good place to steer clear of around Halloween). I've gone swimming (free of charge) in Dollar Lake and decided not to boogie board in Dung Cove, which is not far from Dummy Gillis Lake down Guysborough way.

Anything beginning with East takes up four pages in the gazetteer, and the same is true for North, South, and West. Numbers are pretty popular too. I suppose it's safe to guess that both Eighth Lakes were the eighth lakes discovered on a naming day. There are twelve First Lakes and three Fifth Lakes, in case you were wondering. There are six Five Island Lakes in the book. Why do you suppose that is? Five Acre is a shoal, Five Bridge is a run (brook), Five Eyed Bulls is also a shoal, and Five Finger is a lake. There are rocks, shoals, lakes, islands, and bogs all named Frying Pan, which I suppose is indicative of their shapes.

The G section puts forth a plethora of lakes and rivers named for granite, gulls, geese, and gold.

If you are looking for Hell on Earth, you can find it in a lake, a bay, and a reef, but apparently there is no Heaven in Nova Scotia (alas, John Lennon). However, as everyone knows, you can find Paradise in the Annapolis Valley. Hypocrite Brook runs into the Medway River and Hungry Cove is down by Necum Teuch. There is an ongoing discussion on the internet as to what to call someone from Italy Cross. One droll contributor suggests they should be called Italian Croissants, but I'm not buying in.

There is a Jumping Brook in Inverness County and a Jolly Cliff on Isle Madame. Jim, Joe, Jerome, Jenny, and John all have their own lakes. Joe Tom, however, only has a bog.

Nova Scotia boasts a Kempt Road, a Kempt Shore, a Kempt Head, a Kempt Lake, and a Kempt Brook, but not a single Unkempt place. No doubt there is more than one relaxing cottage on Land of Laziness Lake down by St. Margarets Bay. It is a province of more things "Little" than "Grand": nine Little Harbours, fifty (!) Little Lakes, but only twelve Grand Lakes, and not a single Grand Harbour, although there is a Grandmother Head Lake near

Sherbrooke. "Little" also gets attached to various other bodies of water named for fish, beavers, geese, pine, and ducks. And many, many things are "Long" or "Lower."

The M section of my famous gazetteer reads much like a Cape Breton phone book with the MacKenzies, McIntyres, McLeans, McLeods, and MacPhersons all having many spits, ponds, rivers, and lakes named after them. On a slow day, you might want to drive to Molasses Lake, or, if you're feeling down, get in synch with Moody Brook. If you're in need of cash you could try poking around any of Nova Scotia's three Money Points. Some evening, you might decide to go for a swim at Moon Lake.

When we get to the Ns, down Guysborough way they have a Neverfail Cove, but Chester has a Nevertell Lake not too far away, for those who want to keep their secrets safe. Why someone went to the trouble of naming Nameless Shoal is a bit of a mystery to me.

Oddly enough, there is only one thing (a place) named Oceanview in the gazetteer.

Pinkietown is near Antigonish and there are sixteen Pubnico references.

Quacks Lake is probably named to set it off from the many duck-named lakes previously mentioned, and Quoddy is both a place and a word that means, to some, smoked herring. "Pass the quoddy, please."

I actually swam out to Rat Rock once to watch the seals on a warm summer day, but I can't tell you much about Roaring Bull Rock or even Roaring Cow Shoal. Rocky Lakes are in stiff competition with all the Little Lakes, and are well distributed around the province.

The saints are all properly represented with channels, bays, beaches, islands, rivers, and harbours named for Andrew, Ann,

Bernard, Catherine, George, Margaret, Mary, Francis, Paul, and Peter. Skir Dhu may just mean "black rock" in Gaelic, but it could also be construed as "hidden knife" if not properly pronounced. Sleepy Cove and Sonora sound like relaxing locales, as does Snug Harbour, but watch out for whatever is lurking at Snarl Lake and Snake Spit. And before I leave the S's, may I say how pleased I am that there is now a brewery on Sober Island?

But enough, you say. Too many place names.

It turns out Newfoundland is not the only province with "tickles." We have a passage in Sheet Harbour simply named The Tickles. Twiddling Run is a brook and Tomfool is a shoal. There are brooks, rivers, and lakes named for tomcod, tomahawks, typhus, and tongues.

The U section of the gazetteer is almost entirely reserved for things beginning with Upper, and where there's an Upper, there's usually a Lower, if not a Middle.

The Strait of Canso has an unlikely Venus Cove that may or may not be a nude beach (it is).

Breton Books is the largest publisher in Wreck Cove (okay, the only publisher in Wreck Cove), and way down the eastern shore past Sober Island is Wine Harbour. I must make a point of taking a swim in Whimsical Lake some time when the spirit moves me.

Sadly, there is not a single place name in Nova Scotia that begins with X. I'm hoping that a fan of one of the St. Francis Xavier University X-Men's or X-Women's sports teams one day digs a pond and names it Xavier Pond to help fill the gap.

Along with A Lake, the gazetteer lists a Y Lake, but no other letter-lakes in between, and if it wasn't for the Zwickers and the Zincks, there wouldn't be any place names listed that begin with

Z. But there's my personal alphabetical tour of the land of the *Bluenose*.

I clearly haven't done justice to the wonderful melodic Mi'kmaw names we've inherited—including Antigonish, Ingonish, Merigomish, Musquodoboit, Ecum Secum, Tatamagouche, and many others.

But my gazetteer does not help me solve a place name mystery that has eluded me for decades now. When I first came to this province, I noticed the town name Nancys Cellar on a road map. It was in the dead middle of the province somewhere north of Upper Musquodoboit. It's long gone now from the provincial maps and there's no longer a town of any sort there, if there ever was one. But I always wanted to know the story behind the name. So if anyone has ever been to Nancys Cellar or has a clue as to why it was on the road maps, I'd sure love to know.

MEETING THE *MOLA MOLA*

SHORTLY AFTER NOON ON SEPTEMBER 7, 2017, I WAS FINISHING A bowl of soup and thinking that it was a rather dull day when the phone rang. It was my daughter Sunyata calling to tell me there was some kind of sea creature—a porpoise, perhaps—beached on the rocks near the headland here in Lawrencetown. She had been alerted by a phone call from some animal rescue people who were looking for someone who could check out the situation.

After grabbing our wetsuits, Linda and I jumped in the car and drove through the rain to the ocean. We put on rain gear and walked the perimeter of the headland to see what we could see. We'd been involved in several animal rescue scenarios before and knew full well that sometimes it's possible to help and other times there is absolutely nothing that can be done. But I'm a great supporter of worthy-but-lost causes, and tromping around the headland on this stormy wet day seemed like just the thing to raise my spirits.

We didn't see the creature at first, but soon spotted Sunyata and another good Samaritan down below, beside a truly odd-looking denizen of the deep. It was like nothing I'd ever encountered, and larger than any fish I'd seen in these waters before.

We cautiously scrambled down the slope, sliding in ankle-deep mud, until we reached the rocks below. The tide was out and the "monster" fish was far above the waterline and wedged hopelessly (or so it appeared) between giant boulders.

At this point, there were four of us; Linda and I helped Sunyata, who was trying to get a tarp under the fish. I reckoned it weighed in the range of 160 to 180 kilograms. It was short and squat, taller than it was long, with a very large eye on each side of its head. It immediately reminded me of one of the aliens in the bar scene in the original *Star Wars* movie. Sunyata thought it was some kind of ocean sunfish, but the name didn't seem to fit. I'd never heard of an ocean sunfish, nor had I seen one in my entire aquatic life. Nonetheless, here was a strange and sad creature of the sea in deep trouble. I was afraid it would be impossible for the four of us to heft it back into the sea.

He had a kind of blowhole that we watched carefully as we started throwing water over him (I'll refer to him as a "he" since he had a kind of masculine aura that reminded me of a clueless, well-meaning schoolmate from years gone by who had often been picked on by bullies). We weren't really sure if the poor guy was still alive or not, and all the signs certainly suggested this would be his final resting place. It looked futile.

Strangely, as if all things in life are now recorded for reality television, Andrew Killawee, a cameraman from the *Hope for Wildlife* TV series, appeared and began to film our attempts. We did what we could. We kept splashing our guest with sea water from the pools as we continued to wrestle the tarp beneath him. Eventually we were able to inch him, with great difficulty, back toward the sea—now at least a hundred metres or more from where we stood.

If you haven't found yourself trying to lug an impossibly heavy sea creature while sloshing over seaweed-covered rocks peppered with sharp barnacles, you're probably missing out on one of life's most memorable challenges. But there we were: lugging and lifting and very much hoping he was still alive.

Suddenly the eye blinked and the body heaved. *Splash more water! One, two, three—lift!* Each combined heave moved us mere centimetres toward to the ocean. The wind was roaring and the waves were big, choppy chunks of sea, slamming down before us. We still had no idea what could be done, even if we got the fish into the ocean, and the relentless waves would most certainly drive him back.

Another woman arrived on the scene (I never caught her name—sorry) and joined the effort. More inching forward; more slipping, sliding, scraping on barnacles, and getting cut by the fish's sharp fins. The non-stop rain and wind topped it off, and even though it now seemed hopeless, here we were—trying.

Word had somehow spread, and—lo and behold—I saw Jason Beach from Kannon Beach Surf Shop in Lawrencetown and another lad, both in wetsuits, headed our way. That changed the equation entirely. Soon after, Andrew from MARS (Marine Animal Response Society) arrived. I think he actually said, "Hi, I'm Andrew from MARS. I'll do what I can." Given the fact that our fish buddy definitely looked like an alien, "Andrew from Mars" made perfect sense. It was only later that I realized what "MARS" stood for.

We were now moving forward by metres instead of centimetres. At one time or another each of us slipped and fell under the beast, pinning a leg for a few seconds before the gang lifted again. Once we made it to the waves, Sunyata, Linda, Jason, and

Dan (who turned out to be a surfer from Australia) got our fish into the pounding surf while Andrew and I ran shoreward to put on wetsuits.

By the time we returned, Jason and Dan had our fish out in the waves. We joined them and discussed strategies. Anytime people come together to try to do a good deed for what appears to be a hopeless cause, I am thrilled to be part of that positive human moment; it restores my faith in humanity. This was one of those moments.

The waves pummelled us as the big fish wallowed in the water and we repeatedly lost hold of him. It had become clear that it was not good enough just to heft a fish back into the ocean: he needed to be in deep water. But the waves just kept pushing us back.

Jason and Dan were the most efficient at keeping hold of the beast although they already had cut hands and Dan had a bloody nose. Despite all that, our spirits were high, and it felt like a true communal effort. At this point we were at the very tip of the headland and we needed to go either one way or the other to find deep water. I'm not sure who said it first, but the plan was hatched to lug our friend west, through the belligerent waves, toward Stoney Beach until we rounded the point and could deposit him in the deeper waters of the Lawrencetown River, which spills out into the sea there.

The fish seemed to move occasionally, but he'd been beached for a long time and, assuming he was still even alive, he was obviously exhausted. The waves and wind conspired to exhaust us humans as well. Fortunately, the water was blissfully warm— for Nova Scotia, that is—invariably tempered by those terrifying tropical storms to the south that were ravaging the Caribbean.

Slowly but surely we moved, a strange procession of black-suited humans, half-swimming, half-stumbling through the stormy seas in search of deeper water.

And then suddenly, we were there. No more stones for footholds; fewer waves pounding us back. We'd found the river current moving out to sea. Our fish now quietly slipped below. We treaded water, waiting to see what would happen next. I thought I spotted something farther out, but whatever it was, it quickly vanished.

And that was that. Our hope was that the deeper water, the persistent outgoing current, and the comfort of being back in the sea might all be factors that allowed our guest to survive.

But we'll never know.

As I waded ashore over those slippery barnacled rocks, I had a flashback of Canada Day, many years earlier, when I had brought a drowning woman ashore here at this very location—a drowning woman who did not survive. Those dark and desperate moments never leave you altogether, and they return at such a time as this. The sea is both delightful and deadly. It gives, but it also takes.

But that momentary memory quickly gave way to a kind of damp, fatigued euphoria. A small group of regular folks had come together on this stormy afternoon to try and save a really weird-looking fish—because it seemed like the right thing to do.

And it was.

Back home, after a hot shower, Linda and I both realized we still smelled like fish (the smell would last for a couple of days). A bit of quick research on the internet revealed that my daughter had been right. We had saved (at least I like to believe we saved) a *Mola mola*, often referred to as an ocean sunfish. They mostly live in warmer waters than ours, and I daresay somehow those tropical disturbances sent this guy far northward to us, leaving him weak and stranded and ready to die at Lawrencetown. Adults, apparently, weigh from 250 to 1,000 kilograms. In 1910, one was caught that weighed 1,600 kilograms. That said, ours must have been a baby.

The *Mola mola* is believed to be the heaviest bony fish in the world; their diet consists primarily of jellyfish. They are killed by the thousands, if not millions, each year as bycatch—unwanted fish that die when they are caught accidentally and then are tossed back. In some parts of the world they are finned—their fins are cut off and they are tossed back to sea because they are wrongly considered "bait thieves."

Reading about the *Mola mola* reminded me that we've done some serious damage to the other living beings with which we share this planet, and we should damn well try our best to be kind to our cousins—any opportunity we get.

CHEEZ WHIZ AND BEYOND

THE LABEL ON THE CHEEZ WHIZ JAR THAT RESIDES IN MY refrigerator boasts the product is "Made with Real CHEESE." More startling: it tells me the jar contains "No Artificial Flavours or Colours." And if that isn't enough to warm the cockles of my cheese-loving heart, this particular species of Cheez Whiz has "37% Less Fat Than Regular Cheez Whiz."

I'm somewhat baffled about why the "best-before" date in English is different than the "meilleur-avant" date in French, but I'll let that slide for the moment. I'll also choose to ignore that, in the ingredients list, printed in such a small type it requires a magnifying glass, are salt, calcium chloride, sodium phosphate, corn maltodextrin, and something called "colour." But if the crafty folks at Kraft are not lying to us—all of these items are "natural."

Our old dog Murdo was a big fan of Cheez Whiz—Light or Regular. We'd bought a jar of the gooey orangey paste to encourage him wolf down his pills, which is why it is in our refrigerator. I have to confess, though, in weak moments during an afternoon break from writing or editing, I sometimes sneak down to the kitchen, unearth my hidden box of Vegetable Thins, and chow down on crackers and cheese spread.

Why a grown man who has considerable knowledge of nutrition, healthy eating, and even edible wild plants would do this may seem like a mystery. But the truth is, it reminds me of my childhood.

When I was growing up, my father had a large garden where he grew a dizzying array of vegetables. He had come from a farm family, and his garden provided my mother, brother, and me with corn, tomatoes, eggplant, squash, onions, peas, lima beans, and much more. My mother froze much of it and we'd eat daily from the freezer through the colder months. So, generally, we had a pretty healthy diet.

But like any family of the time, we were bombarded with unreliable information about what was "good for us," so I have fond memories of many supermarket items that came in cans, jars, and plastic containers. In those days, a healthy snack was Cheez Whiz on celery, although I doubt the Cheez Whiz back then was quite up to twenty-first-century standards. Still, it was fatty and gooey and it more or less tasted like something related to cheese.

My father was a fan of corned beef from a tin, because that had been a comfort food to him when he'd been a soldier during the Second World War. Stationed near Cambridge, England, he'd helped send fellow soldiers off to Germany in great bombers to do damage to the enemy. So we ate our fair share of tinned beef, which contained a considerable amount of salt.

I also admit I had a boyhood love of Spam. Yes, Spam. In those days, it did not refer to unwanted emails, but was some kind of meat product. It came in a can (and still does) with a nifty little key for unravelling a strip of the actual can in order to get at the meat—or whatever it was. I used to save the little keys as a child, thinking they were somehow magical.

I can still envision the ritual of opening the can and watching the oddly shaped blob of Spam plop onto the cutting board. I loved nothing more than a fried Spam sandwich. My mother would cut the blob into small slabs and throw them in the frying pan with a little Crisco. The Crisco was probably unnecessary since the Spam had enough fat to fry itself nicely, but my mom was a fan of Crisco, which was purportedly the first shortening made entirely of vegetable oil. It had been around since 1911 so it had proven itself reliable many times over in North American homes. My grandmother had taught my mom to use Crisco, forsaking all other forms of fat used for cooking.

In the end, my mother would produce a fried Spam sandwich: a hunk of Spam lodged between two flawless slices of white Wonder Bread slathered with mayonnaise and mustard. It makes my mouth water just to think about it.

It is worth noting that I am not alone in my nostalgic appreciation of some of the highly processed and largely unhealthy prepared and canned foods that still linger on our shelves. I was pleased to discover from a hasty Google search that in 2014 there was a competition for the best Spam recipe at the North Carolina State Fair. Moreover, the UK celebrates an annual Spam Appreciation Week. I kid you not.

I recall mustard sandwiches as well. Yes—just white bread and mustard. Or, in a pinch, just mayonnaise and the two uniform white slices. For most of my life I was afraid to think too much about what mayonnaise really was, until I actually made some with eggs and oil and a few other ingredients. The result was less than successful, though, because it turns out fats and oils don't actually mix very well.

And that's why mayonnaise manufacturers add EDTA. *What*

is EDTA? you may ask. It stands for ethylenediaminetetraacetic acid. It allows the oils and fats to get along quite nicely, producing the Hellmann's and even the Miracle Whip we know and love. According to the Eating Real Food website, however, although EDTA is considered safe as a food additive, it is a "persistent organic pollutant. It resists degradation from biological, chemical, and photolytic processes," which does not sound good for the planet.

My mother, who considered herself a "modern woman" of her generation, was subjected daily to various forms of brainwashing through product advertisements in *Redbook* and *Ladies' Home Journal* and via commercials on TV.

Against my father's wishes, she stopped buying butter for a while in favour of its supposedly healthier substitute, margarine. No matter how many adamant actors on TV said that it tasted "just like butter," it never did. Ultimately, butter was vindicated and was returned to the table in our house by the twenty-first century. Eggs were never removed from the family diet, I might add, even during those dark days when they were sometimes accused of clogging our arteries and shortening our lives.

I realize I've only barely touched upon the gastronomic nostalgia of my generation, and I should add that none of the abovementioned products ever killed anyone I knew personally. All of the preservatives in our processed foods prevented us from getting food poisoning, I suppose, and for that, we should be thankful. I've only had food poisoning once in my life; I got it by eating some stewed tomatoes from a can I'd left open in the fridge for a couple of weeks. The result was not pretty, and it involved considerable carpet cleaning.

I am, these days, mostly an advocate of healthy organic eating. I could wax on about kale and Swiss chard right here, but

I'll save that for another essay. So here's a final note about an old standby that we all know and love: peanut butter. Skippy would have been the Cadillac of peanut butters in my day, but you'll find none of it in my house now. Instead, I have jar of organic peanut butter that Murdo and I dipped into from time to time. The oil in it separates from the brown mass (no EDTA, I suppose) and rises to the top, but that doesn't bother me, and it didn't seem to bother Murdo. The only problem is that I've been keeping it for the last three months in the cupboard where I would traditionally keep peanut butter—and as part of my research as I wrote this piece, I decided to read the label. It most emphatically stated: "Refrigerate after opening." On top of that, the best-before date in both English and French reveals I should have tossed it about six months ago.

And yet, I survive to tell the tale. Considering this and all the garbage I put into my digestive system as a kid, I guess philosopher Friedrich Nietzsche's quote applies: "That which does not kill us makes us stronger."

THE JOYS AND SORROWS OF NOVA SCOTIA COASTAL GARDENING

MY LITTLE PATCH OF SOIL AND I GO BACK TO 1978. IT WAS ON a piece of land that had been farmed and forgotten, and I was more than ready to test the will of a North Atlantic summer and woo the land to bring forth food for the table. Over these more than forty years I've met my farming failures head-on, but still, as yet another planting season approaches, I am filled with a blind optimism that never ceases to amaze me.

The garden is on the edge of Lawrencetown Marsh, a long stone's throw from the sea that rules the seasons here and tests my heady optimism each summer. When I first moved here, I used an old Rototiller my father had given me to loosen the soil and give me my start. It was challenged by the abundance of stones that jammed its claws, and eventually it succumbed to rust and age, as so many of us do. But it served me well and often reminded me of my father's gardening days, and of my own links to my farming ancestry.

I always, always, tilled too soon and planted too early. Thus, my first round of seeds was doomed to rot in the cold, wet ground, and if anything sprouted, the spindly seedlings would be far too discouraged by what they saw to ever find the courage to grow to fruition. But with each successive spring, I would fall under the delusion that *this* year the warmth of summer would come sooner than ever before, and perhaps I'd at least have an early harvest of spinach.

To prepare the garden, I haul seaweed in the winter to help fertilize the ground. In February, the frozen heaps of the stuff piled in my garden and covered in snow prompt neighbours to ask me if there are dead animals in there. By spring, however, the seaweed thaws and rots, and then Kenny Crowell of Crowell Road comes with his trusty tractor and plows it under. Once it has all been turned over, I stand there at sunset and just stare at the beautifully exposed soil, smell its richness, and envision the harvests that could be. But nowadays I wait until May—finally held back by reason—to begin the first planting.

The first crop to harvest is, of course, rocks. No matter how many thousands of stones I've lifted and tossed into the marsh, there are always more, planted by the devil, some say, to remind me that farming in Nova Scotia should not be easy.

I'm descended from several generations of farmers, so it's in my blood, you see. It connects me to my father and grandfather and the men before them who tilled softer soil than this to feed their many children. I feel that connection as I begin to form rows for seed planting. I feel it in my feet and hands, and something happens in my mind—a primitive directive linking humans to dirt in ways we should not forget.

In the summer of 2016 the soil was wet and heavy, a reluctant host even to lowly radishes. But then it went dry for nearly two months: dry and dusty and refusing to allow anything to grow.

Each year seemed to provide some extreme: too wet, too dry, too cold, then too hot (for spinach and lettuce, at least). Fog sometimes lingered through June and July.

Ultimately, however, as each season progresses, there is reason for hope. The chives are up and thriving. The kale has inched its way skyward. A few red radishes reluctantly grow round and fat. I can pinch a small leaf from the long-awaited spinach straight from the soil and drop it into my mouth, savouring the very dirt on my tongue.

Alas, I've given up on peas. The pheasants watch me plant them from the nearby marsh grass and, not long after I leave the garden, they scratch them out, one by one, and eat them all. Should any have been missed, they finish the job as soon as a single leaf breaks the soil. The same holds true for beans. Once upon a time I could toddle down to my garden on a fine July day and feast on raw peas straight from the pod and green beans snapped from the vine. But the rising pheasant population has curtailed those pleasures. I admitted defeat to the pheasants long ago.

But not all the birds molest my garden. I've had the most interesting encounters while working alone there: gulls stealing sandwiches, ducks with trailing ducklings in the nearby pools, the snake-like sounds of bitterns in the bulrushes. I've seen chickadees and full-throated song sparrows, geese honking from high above, herons spearing minnows in the brook, hawks cruising for mice, eagles flapping through the heavens, and barn swallows swooping by my ear like *Star Wars* Starfighters.

I recall one amazing afternoon: I was working the late spring soil when a cattle egret landed in my garden, just an arm's length away, and shadowed me for nearly an hour as I fashioned new rows for planting. The next day I learned that an old friend, the poet Alden Nowlan, had died in hospital in New Brunswick at that very hour.

So, despite the setbacks and challenges, the garden remains a sacred place for me—and always will.

But as gardening season progresses, as the days get (somewhat) warmer and the harsh winds subside, one must confront the demons of weeds. Apparently, the harvested seaweed harbours the exotic and ambitious seeds of wild plants from near and far. Many of the weeds are edible: dandelion, pigweed (more politely known as lamb's quarters), plantain (if your palette is willing), various wild forms of mustard, camomile to calm the gardener's frayed nerves, and many more. All should be welcome, I suppose, but many have a habit of taking over the place if they're given a chance to go to seed or to spread their despicable roots.

But there will be no pesticides or herbicides for me and my garden plot, thank you. Instead, I weed by hand and hoe. I make verbal claims that I like weeding; that it breeds patience and discipline. And there *is* something noble to be said for dirt under the nails. Weed-wrestling is not for everyone, I admit, but it has its moments. My sad confession, however, is that by August, the weeds always win. Well, the weeds and the dill. Yes, herb aficionados, you heard me correctly. Each year I have more dill in my garden than you'd find in a respectable pickle factory. It grows tall, aromatic, and elegant. It's so delightful to look at that I tend to leave it be. But it does eventually drop innumerable seeds. The pheasants like them, but they don't eat enough to prevent the dill from coming back year after year in overabundance.

I've learned to accept what works and what doesn't in my coastal garden. I can't grow cauliflower, cabbage, or broccoli—that's all there is to it. I would if I could, but it seems to require either real pesticides or that I go down there and spray them with soapy water every other day, and I'm just not up for that. I can wrestle a few sprigs of parsley out of the soil, but it grows so slowly that sometimes the weeds choke it out before it can supply me with greens for tabbouleh.

Lettuce grows green and leafy and even likes the fog, but it goes tall and seedy by early August and I have to settle for kale. When I first started growing kale I was very proud of my harvest and I fed my family numerous concoctions made of kale—until rebellion set in. My kids threatened to uproot the crunchy vitamin-filled green in the night, but I promised to stop inventing new kale dishes and started feeding it to the much-more-grateful neighbour's horse. You've probably noticed that, in recent years, kale has become increasingly fashionable. Who could have guessed? Knowing almost anyone can grow kale almost anywhere with almost no attention, I find myself reluctant to pay exorbitant restaurant prices for a kale salad. That just doesn't seem kosher. But still, I am fond of kale and I'll eat it raw or cooked.

I can usually coax a single crop of spinach out of my coastal garden; I like to savour it raw in salads. I don't cook it, though, because it seems like half-acre of spinach boils down to a single paltry cup of wilted greens. Popeye would not be impressed.

Radishes, as mentioned, will grow in earnest until they literally explode in their skins. There's nothing quite like the first red radish of the year, and I'm opposed, on principle, to all the different colours of radishes out there these days. But then, after the first four radishes of the season—well, that's probably enough.

Garlic seems to grow in my patch. And leeks. Long live the underappreciated leek. I bought at least a hundred baby leek transplants on sale in the Annapolis Valley last year. Due to the dry months, they did nothing but look at me sadly and tell me they didn't think they liked it here. But the ones with the fortitude to survive past the drought started growing like heroes late into the fall, and after they were plucked from the soil and sautéed, they tasted delicious. I even transplanted a few to live in the house, where they continued to prosper. Who would have thought that leeks make fine houseplants?

I've experimented with seeds and transplants of some of the more "exotic" varieties of vegetables sold in the garden stores. Kohlrabi grew just fine, but eating it was too much like chewing lumber. Perhaps beavers would enjoy munching on it, but I didn't. One rather pro-kohlrabi website boasts: "It's a fantastically versatile vegetable with a taste and texture somewhere between cabbage and broccoli stems." But how often do you really feel like eating broccoli stems? Various other exotic seeds just didn't have the backbone to flourish here in the north, so I've ceased experimenting with them as well.

I haven't yet mentioned the rabbits or, of course, the deer. The rabbits are large: Arctic hares, to be specific. They like lawn grass, which is fine, but have also developed a taste for lettuce, spinach, and parsley—none of which I would assume are part of their diet on the Arctic tundra, where their ancestors once lived.

By late August, if I am lucky, I sometimes have one or two pale green tomatoes. I've tried every variety out there and all have failed, including the variety called Siberian tomatoes. Yes, Siberian. The plants were robust and produced large, exceptionally heavy, Soviet-looking tomatoes. The only problem was, they never ripened. Much like the kohlrabi, they were aggressively hard and unfriendly to the taste buds, so I gave up on them. I've discovered that the tiny cherry tomatoes survive best—"Sweet

Millions," I think they are called.

The Sweet Millions are indeed tasty, but these baby tomatoes often fall prey to slugs. I wish I could say I was friend to one and all in the animal kingdom, but I draw the line at slugs. If I could sacrifice a handful of tomatoes to the little slimy buggers, I would happily do so, but they seem to want the whole crop, eating part of one here and part of another there, leaving their slime to create a mass of rotting goo where there should be luscious red tomatoes.

I've heard that skunks eat slugs, which is one potential solution, but I've had my issues with skunks in the past, so I can't be persuaded to adopt a family of skunks and post them near my garden.

I also know you can put out an ice cube tray filled with beer and the slugs will crawl in, presumably to get drunk, and then drown. But beer is expensive and I think beer suicide is just a bit too good for these suckers. I prefer to pick them up and toss them high and away from the garden, but if I happen to go away for a week late in the season and no one is willing to stand in as a slug-tosser for me, the slugs always win out.

Zucchini grows well in my garden. Too well, in fact. I plant way too many zucchini seeds and the pheasants don't seem to care for them. Slugs are not fans of zukes, and the rabbits don't seem to know what to make of them. So, later in August, the zucchini squash want to take over the whole garden—they even bully out the weeds. They have exorbitant flowers, long vines, and big leaves (where the slugs hide from the sun). And before you know it, I have dozens of zucchinis on my hands, many the size of oblong watermelons. I know they should be harvested while they're young, but they seem to mutate from mild little pickle-sized squash into bloated, weapon-like vegetables overnight. I give them away to my neighbours until they stop answering the doorbell when I ring—so if you're hoping to make a decade's supply of zucchini bread this summer, just drop me a line.

I planted some Jerusalem artichokes on the edge of my garden one year and was thrilled at the tall yellow crowd of flowers that emerged by September. Unfortunately, there was no stopping them after that, and they continue to spread like wildfire in and around the garden. I remember waking up one fine September morning to see that the Jerusalem artichokes had bloomed overnight for the first time, and to my groggy mind and unfocussed eyes it looked like someone had parked a school bus in the marsh.

Toward the end of the season, I'm always hoping a few of the many pumpkin seeds I've planted will produce plants that yield one or two sizable pumpkins. I've bought those expensive monster pumpkin seeds on occasion, but they just aren't that ambitious in my patch of ground. If I do achieve a few modest jack-o'-lantern–sized pumpkins, I yank them from the vine as quickly as I can, because the neighbourhood pheasants like to peck them open and eat the tasty seeds inside, leaving the orange orb to rot in the late summer sun.

But let me end on an upbeat note. Aside from legendary kale crops, I can also grow lush knee-high plants of Swiss chard. I don't know if Swiss chard has the same nutritional credentials as kale, but for me it's high up on my list. Red or green Swiss chard grows through most of the summer, and I believe a good feed of Swiss chard can cure whatever modern malaise might inflict your twenty-first–century soul. Raw, sautéed, boiled, lasagna-ed, stir-fried, fricasseed, or tossed into a ragout, Swiss chard can satisfy your craving for green and take you to a happy place.

And oddly enough, the deer, out of sympathy (and respect for me as a gardener, I believe), leave the chard alone. They eat the leaves off the zucchini plants, dig up the beets (yes, I can grow beets!), tromp on the Sweet Millions that survive the slugs, and rip up the parsley by the roots. But they leave the Swiss chard alone until the first frost of the year. Then, invariably, they forget about their compassion for me and mow the chard to the ground— usually all in one night.

I always forgive them for it. Aside from the slugs, in fact, I forgive all the wild things that invade my garden and rob me of sustenance. We've taken a fair bit from them over the centuries, and I'm happy to oblige by giving a little back.

THE PHILOSOPHY OF SNOW

MY WIFE, LINDA, WAS A BIT PUZZLED ON A COLD DAY NEAR THE end of 2015 when she saw me out in the yard shovelling snow off the grass. There was still plenty of ice and snow in the driveway and on the path to the house, so it didn't quite make sense to her that I was shovelling snow off the lawn. But then, she has grown somewhat accustomed to watching me do things which, on the surface, seem illogical. Usually there is an explanation, but not always.

In this case, it was perfectly reasonable—and, if I may say so, thoughtful. You see, a warm fall and a mild December meant the grass underneath was still green. I had been wandering around the yard elsewhere and discovered a patch where some animal, presumably one of our Arctic hares, had cleared the snow away in order to chow down on the grass. So I was just trying help them out by providing easy access to their lawn buffet. Surely the hares and the deer (who consume my garden in summer and the shrubs come winter) would appreciate my efforts.

When I'd immigrated to Canada (to Nova Scotia, really) in 1978 and moved into a rented house in Seaforth, outside Halifax, I hadn't realized I was in for a surprise. In the morning after my first real Canadian snowstorm, I was alarmed to discover that my old, rusty Toyota appeared to be missing from my driveway. I assumed it had been stolen until I ventured out into the head-high snowdrift to discover that the car had simply been buried, not stolen at all. This was my first hint that a Canadian winter was a beast I was truly not familiar with. But I grew to accept, if not appreciate, the season for its several virtues.

Linda bought us snowshoes for Christmas in 2015, despite global warming, so we're hoping for a few good winter slammers yet, I guess, before things warm up too much. But I'm not totally optimistic for the long run. I've become one of those old geezers who pontificates about how winter is no longer what it used to be.

The previous year had been a fat bastard of a season. Winter had really arrived in February, with snow and heavy rain and a flash freeze. We were burdened with moving from a house we owned in Bedford to our new home in East Lawrencetown, and winter definitely had it in for us. There was snow and ice, then melting, then more snow and ice. It was winter agony all around and dirty snow piles lingered in grocery store parking lots until April. So yes, winter can still be reasonably apocalyptic if it wants to be.

Nonetheless, we should not write off the potential splendour of winter. It was probably Farley Mowat who first drew my attention to the poetics of snow, writing in *The Snow Walker* that, on any given day, snow is falling somewhere in the world, and it can be found "climbing in scimitar drifts to wall up doors and windows of farmhouses" or "whirling fiercely over the naked sweep of a frozen plain." As I became more and more Canadian, I began to see the visual and metaphorical beauty of snow.

But after doing extensive research for my book *Nova Scotia: Shaped by the Sea*, I was mightily glad I hadn't been living in Nova

Scotia ten thousand years ago, during one of the several ice ages. At some point back then, the snow that had fallen (and fallen and fallen) compacted itself into ice—much like the damn stuff I had to chisel and chip with a spade and an axe off my deck last winter. In those ancient times, the ice built up until it was a few kilometres thick, and stretched all the way to Sable Island. The sledding would have been good in those days and the snowshoes would certainly have come in handy, but the rabbits would not have found me out in my yard trying to clear a spot for them to nibble on a tasty bit of grass, I am sure.

Sometimes, when I think of winter during the summer, I can only remember the glazed windshield of my car. I grow sullen at such moments, unable to remember the golden moments of hiking through the snowy woods, or tobogganing with my kids, or learning to snowboard on a hill overlooking the sea. Ice, of course, is worse than snow, and I should keep it in an altogether separate category, but I can't. For us here in Nova Scotia, ice and snow are close cousins—like rowdy farm boys from the Valley, out to cause mayhem.

During those dark summer moments I realize the warmth will not last and, all too soon, I will be back in my driveway on a blustery morning with an automobile totally encased in a thick layer of snow beneath a dense veneer of ice. I'll have to do battle to somehow break open the frozen door. Once opened, it will not close properly, and I'll have to tie it to my elbow with a bungee cord as I drive, but not before I tackle the windshield with its inch-thick plating of ice, and wiper blades immobilized beyond hope. At such moments of dark reminiscence, winter represents only pain and despair, and there is no poetry in snow or in any other aspect of the damnable season.

One recent Christmas, however, there was no snow. Temperatures rose to near-record highs as Linda and I sat on our ice-free deck in beach attire, sipping wine and watching the sun go down. But on that day, no one in my family or in the neighbourhood was foolhardy enough to say out loud, "It looks like it's going to be an easy winter." No—not by a long shot. You just don't do that in Nova Scotia. Ever.

When I first began to study early Canadian literature, I discovered a common theme in the novels: if you were going to die in Canadian fiction, the preferred means was to freeze to death. Although it seemed like a bit of a cliché after several books, I realized it just came with the territory and was highly realistic. Getting eaten by bears came in a distant second for tragic endings for protagonists, and was more dramatic, but a snowy wilderness death was what most authors favoured to close a good tragic tale. I should note that, in English literature, there was hardly ever a story with characters who froze to death. They just didn't have the right climate, so authors were forced to invent other ways to kill off their characters.

I have fully tried to embrace winter over the years as best I can. This, of course, includes winter surfing, which sometimes means paddling in the ocean with slush and ice-bobbing dovekies. It was never more invigorating and inspiring than the time I caught a crisp North Atlantic head-high wave and skidded across its exquisite wall while being pelted in the face with ice pellets from an ambitious north wind.

Shovelling hillocks of snow from the driveway is, for the most part, not much fun. It kills people sometimes, so it's best to avoid it if you can. I stopped complaining too much about our winter here, though, after a foray to Happy Valley, Labrador, one

May, where I saw a man in his front yard with a lawnmower. Although it was relatively warm day, the snow in his yard was still several feet deep and he was attempting to get rid of it by mowing it.

I'm pretty sure he wasn't doing it for the rabbits. He was likely fed up with winter hanging on so long, so he thought he'd chop up its remnants with his lawnmower blade. He wanted his damn lawn back. Although his efforts were heroic, they did not appear to be successful. Worse, his neighbours were laughing at him.

So I reckon our winters are not really so bad. I was reminded of Happy Valley one recent winter when I found a neighbour down the road attacking the ice on his driveway with a chainsaw. But let's hope that winter was a fluke—nature's brave and heroic last hurrah before turning Nova Scotia into the land of the palm trees.

If the day arrives when we no longer have snow, I will miss it—I really will. Nonetheless, imprinted on my brain forever is the image of a coastal headland, a beautiful, truncated drumlin left here as a gift from those glaciers of long, long ago, bleached white by fresh winter snow and gleaming in the distance at sunset. If that were to become only a memory, I would feel the loss most deeply.

POTHOLES ARE THE NEXT BIG THING

ILIVE ON LESLIE ROAD NEAR LAWRENCETOWN BEACH AND LATELY my road has become somewhat famous for the abundance of potholes. In fact, we are under consideration for the dubious title of "Worst Road in Atlantic Canada."

Most folks would find such an accolade disconcerting, but I like to look at it another way: with snow and rain falling from the sky at regular (i.e., daily) intervals, I like to think that the pothole is not half empty, but half full. I don't know where the "Best Road in Atlantic Canada" is, and I don't really care. "Worst Road" sounds much more interesting, and indeed this one is interesting.

A few years back, I phoned the local Department of Transportation office in Chezzetcook about the poor condition of Leslie Road. The man who answered the phone—Dave, I think—said that, because of the season, nothing could be done. That was during the spring, I believe. (Neighbours reported they received the same response in the summer, so presumably fall and winter also offer impediments to pothole repair.) Not one to take things lying down, I asked if they could send a truck to dump some small piles of gravel along the road, and told them I would gladly volunteer to head out with a shovel and fill the holes in for fun.

Dave laughed and suggested I was scamming him to get free gravel for my driveway. He said people on the Eastern Shore tried to scam his office for free gravel all the time. Clearly, he thought I was a crank. I could not convince him I'd enjoy getting some fresh air and exercise while doing a good deed by filling potholes. He also said if I got caught filling the potholes by his workers, it would lead to labour issues and union grievances.

So now it's spring again, the road is the worst it's ever been, and we are finally getting the recognition we deserve. This morning I did a quick count and found that, on average, there are two to five potholes (no exaggeration) for each metre of Leslie Road. Leslie Road is 2.1 kilometres long. That would suggest there are between 4,200 and 10,500 potholes altogether (and I'm not even going to count the minor indentations with aspirations to one day be counted with their more sizable brethren).

I am thinking of buying a couple of truckloads of really good gravel on my own and going at this as a community service anyway. Sure, I'll miss the crazy car dance we all do as we attempt to weave around the larger chasms on this muddy track that looks like a war zone. The good news is that everyone drives slowly, sparing the pheasants and chipmunks that cross our paths, so in some ways, it would be sad to see things change.

Unfortunately, I've been informed that weight restrictions are in effect right now in Nova Scotia, so dump trucks are not allowed to drive here on any paved road.

But I'm sure there is a way to turn this all around. Eventually the trucks with gravel will roll again. And if I think personal pothole repair would be a fun thing, maybe other people out here will as well. It will be warmer in Nova Scotia soon, and with tourism lagging these days, I propose that those of us on Leslie

Road (and people along other potholed boulevards) lure tourists for a specialized vacation that involves pothole repair (given that many folks from the US and Europe live in urban areas where they never see real *quality* potholes).

I'm sure at least some of these deprived tourists would jump at the chance to travel to Lawrencetown Beach for a little outdoor exercise. Instead of coming here to gamble, or eat lobster, or surf, or chase whales and puffins, they'd come and pay good money to fill our potholes. Anyone could do it, young or old. It would be good, healthy exercise in clean salt air near the sea. Travellers could bring their own shovels, or I could rent them one from my shed.

Scoff all you like. I think it's the next big thing.

RESPECTABLE

ONCE UPON A TIME I WAS NOT RESPECTABLE. IN MY LONG-GONE hippie days, I had grown my hair long, shaved biweekly, wore sandals, had poor posture, and often seemed to have a grudge against much of the respectable world. I had worked hard at developing an aura that clearly established that I was not part of the Establishment.

But that was then and this is now. The clock has been ticking and times have changed. Not long ago, I was walking into a store—one of those so-called "dollar stores" where almost nothing actually costs a single loonie (and where, despite the sign that says something like DollarWorld or DollarDreams or DollarHeaven or DollarEverything, the typical price inside seems to be $2.50). But I was going in to buy a pair of reading glasses—so-called "designer glasses"—that sold for $5.00 (this, despite the fact that I have a drawer full of reading glasses, none of which seem to be quite right for reading).

At any rate, I was walking into the store as a really rough-looking young man was walking out. At first glance, he looked like some kind of biker—not the lawyer-who's-a-weekend-Harley-Davidson-wannabe-biker kind, but the real McCoy. A true

Hells Angels–type. He had a tattoo on his forehead that appeared to be in Russian, he had a ripped-up black leather jacket, long spaghetti-like strands of black hair, and he was built like a grizzly bear. I wasn't exactly afraid of him, but the fight-or-flight part of my brain had an escape route already in mind should he suddenly pull a jagged hunting knife from his belt.

No knife emerged, though, and, instead, he did the darndest thing. He held the door open for me, nodded (respectfully!), and said something like, "How are ya, sir?"

I smiled politely and would have tipped my hat, had I been wearing one. He walked off and I went about my business.

As I browsed through thousands of items I had no interest in buying, I could hear my mother's voice reminding me as a little boy that I should not judge people by their appearance. "Yes, Mom, I know that," I answered in my head. "I am, after all, an adult." Then a darker thought—this time in my own inner voice—reminded me that the biker/Samaritan had judged *me* by my appearance. He had deemed me older and, God help me, respectable. Respectable, despite the fact that my hair was still (somewhat) long, I was unshaven, I wore sandals, had poor posture, and still had a grudge against much of the respectable world.

How could such a thing have happened?

I picked up a new pair of reading glasses with ridiculous shiny purple frames and the young lady at the cash register asked, "Did you find everything you were looking for, Sir?"—driving home the reminder of my respectability. I paid with a credit card, silly me, and then left, opening my own door this time.

Before I drove off, I sat in my car, looking across the highway at the lineup of idling cars waiting to get to the drive-thru window at Tim Hortons. I suddenly felt nostalgic for those days of yesteryear when I was not (at least in appearance) the slightest bit respectable in the eyes of the adult world.

When I was twenty years old, my hair had cascaded down my back to well below my shoulder blades. As David Crosby had advised, I was letting my freak flag fly. My jeans were ripped in several important places, decades before this became fashionable. I drove a beat-up black 1959 Volkswagen I had bought from a girl at my university for fifty dollars because she wasn't able to get it started (all it needed was a good push from a couple of bearded friends and a pop of the clutch).

In any given conversation, you could hear me complain about some disagreeable thing as being a "hassle." I didn't trust police—or, really, anyone with any authority—and for some completely unknown reason, I had a chip on my shoulder the size of a boom box against what we called "The Establishment." I was not particularly polite to anyone unless they appeared to be older than seventy. Apparently, I felt a kinship to really old people but mistrusted most anyone between thirty and sixty-nine, except for certain radical authors and rabble-rousing rock musicians. In my own mind, I was not respectable and would never join the rotten ranks of those who were.

As a result of my look and my attitude, I was indeed "hassled"—often. In a department store where I went to buy records (Frank Zappa, Quicksilver Messenger Service, Ultimate Spinach), security guards would follow me, expecting me to shoplift. I had friends who did just that, arguing they were "liberating" the records, not stealing. I chided them for stealing and would not break my own code of ethics, but I did sometimes confront the security guards defensively and ask them why they were spying on me. Usually they just shook their heads and walked away.

At the bank where I had a savings account, the clerk often viewed me with suspicion. I would get funny looks from middle-aged women and business-suited men. I assumed they thought I was there to rob the bank, or at least to swindle it in some way. Whenever I tried to deposit a paycheque from my nursing home janitorial job, the teller would tell me they'd have to hold it for seven business days before I could withdraw any cash. This, despite the fact that I had at least that much already in the account because I was saving up to buy a new surfboard.

But I guess the ultimate proof of my cultivated disrespect-ability was how often I was stopped in my beloved fifty-buck Beetle by the police. I actually did not use the term "pigs" in those days, but I understood what my hairy brothers meant when they used that cliché.

I suppose the cops expected to find me high on drugs or transporting weapons to fringe radical meetings, planning the overthrow of the government. I was always self-righteous and somewhat snarly, and asked why it was *me* who was stopped. Was it because of the way I looked?

"Of course not," they would answer as I slowly handed over my driver's license—and my long hair began to stream out the window in the wind. "Your tail light is out. You should get it fixed." I wasn't even sure the car had ever had working tail lights, but I would remain indignant. Amazingly, the police officers who stopped me almost never got riled, and almost never gave me a ticket. In my steamy, convoluted, self-righteous little brain, I was actually somewhat disappointed. If the police were really out to get me, why didn't they flat-out arrest me and throw me in jail for looking and being so disrespectable? That would have proven a thing or two, and would have shored up my beliefs about the hated "Establishment." But then, the world just didn't always make sense to me back then.

Eventually I grew older, slightly less hairy, and somewhat less angry. Slowly but surely, the clerks at the liquor store stopped asking to see any ID. Such requests had continued until I was past thirty, much to my delight. I began to confront smiling tellers at the bank, and eventually men who looked like criminals were opening doors for me. Apparently, this is what happens to a good lot of us as we age.

Young punks occasionally sneer at me, but kids show relatively little contempt for those my age these days, even though my generation has robbed those younger than me of job prospects and natural resources, and has given them global warming, high taxes, and mind-numbing communication devices.

And so, dear friends, I have now settled into respectability, although it still doesn't quite feel right. Perhaps my youthful instincts were right, though, and something will happen when I turn seventy. I'll let my hair grow even longer, shave even less, rip my jeans in some unfashionable way, and find new and creative ways to flout authority.

It sounds like a lot more fun than going quietly into that good night.

LETTER TO CANADA

D EAR CANADA,

First off, let me thank you for taking me in. In 1978, I was a restless and rebellious young man living in New Jersey, looking for some other place in the world where I could feel more at home. I'd spent time in Nova Scotia already and it seemed like a haven from much of what I thought was wrong with the world: crime, corruption, consumerism, pollution, blind patriotism, and paranoia.

And it was just that. To some degree, it still is. But I was an idealist then, and today I am more of a realist. We've gradually been infected here in Nova Scotia by those things on my list, but we haven't been overrun by them, so we'll need to be vigilant.

As I discovered in the mid-1970s, in order to live in Nova Scotia I had to become an immigrant to Canada. Canadian immigration turned me down for two years running, and I couldn't figure out why Canada didn't want me. I was young, educated, fairly bright (in a goofy head-in-the-clouds sort of way), ambitious, and healthy. Despite all that, it looked fairly certain that Canada would never let me in. I simply wasn't wanted.

The explanation was that I would be taking a job away from a Canadian. The rule at the time was this: I had to be able to prove I had a job skill no other Canadian possessed. At the time, I had schooled myself in low-tech "alternative" energy: passive solar, wind, biomass, and such. I even had a job offer from a small Nova Scotian firm.

Nope, Canada is not for you, the form letter said.

But I was persistent, and eventually was granted an interview at the consulate in Manhattan—in the Exxon Building, if I remember correctly. I even got a haircut and borrowed some shine-able shoes for the event, I was trying that hard.

The consulate official who interviewed me kept asking me why a young, educated, fairly bright, ambitious, and healthy young man would want to move to Nova Scotia, for God's sake. It seemed he viewed the province as a backwater, a lacklustre place, but he admitted he'd never been there. I gave him my reasons and he still shook his head. But as he stared at my rather thick file of documents and letters which had been building up for two years, he finally just threw up his hands, admitted he still didn't "get it," and signed the paper saying I would be allowed to move to Canada. (He still thought I should reconsider the Nova Scotia part.)

And that was it. I was in. I became a landed immigrant and a few years later took a test to see if I was worthy of citizenship. One of the questions was this: "What level of government collects the garbage?" I nailed the quiz and found myself swearing allegiance to the Queen. Really? Canada has a queen? Well, what the heck.

It all worked out rather nicely.

Like so many other immigrants I had this wonderfully positive view of the country and the people. I still have that today.

So thank you, Canada. You reluctantly took me in, allowed me to write books and travel the country, gave me a teaching job, and provided a damn fine place to raise kids. (*You mean the country pays you to have children?* Well, yeah, sort of. *Holy mackerel!*) You did that and more for me. Thank you, Canada.

Okay, I'm gushing. It's not exactly what I meant to say.

For the record, Canada, let me say the whole "Canada 150" thing seemed a bit, um, artificial. There's evidence that early peoples were living in Debert well over ten thousand years ago. Let's start planning for Nova Scotia's eleven thousandth birthday now, maybe. That would be a blast. Also, I am well aware that many other Indigenous peoples across this vast land can trace their ancestors even farther back. In April 2017, for example, archeologists on Triquet Island in British Columbia found artifacts from a village that was fourteen thousand years old.

Just a few years before 1867, most Nova Scotians, including Joe Howe, were opposed to Confederation, but through some fancy political finagling on the part of Charlie Tupper (then the premier of Nova Scotia) the province was signed up anyway. And that's probably been a good move, because it prevented this fair province from being absorbed by the Americans.

But today there is still a lot to celebrate. The whole "150" thing may have been a bit of a gimmick, but I'd rather not fight it and instead find other, more significant ways to give the true ancestors of this land the respect they deserve.

In 1995 Cynthia Good, an editor at Penguin Books, asked me to contribute to a book she was putting together called *If You Love This Country*. Other contributors included former prime minister Joe Clark, journalist Peter C. Newman, musician Stompin' Tom Connors, and astronaut Dr. Roberta Bondar. Around that time it appeared that Quebec was going to leave Canada, and this book was a kind of communal plea to Quebecers to stay with us—please.

I wrote about my recent author tour of the lower North Shore of Quebec, from Sept-Îles to Blanc-Sablon. Early on, I discovered that the farther away I travelled from the urban cores of Canada (Toronto, Ottawa, etc.), the more Canadian everything felt. That was especially true of Harrington Harbour, Aylmer Sound, and Tête-à-la-Baleine. But it was in a motel room in Blanc-Sablon, just shy of the Labrador border, where I had the most Canadian experience: my Québécois host snuck into my room at night while I was sleeping and positioned a stuffed seven-foot black bear in an attack posture.

When I awoke in the morning, there was the threatening bear, seemingly ready to pounce. It was a joke, of course, and a good one. Everyone at the motel who knew about the prank was hoping I (a "southerner") would wake up with an ear-piercing scream, scared out of my pyjamas. But, for some reason, I didn't. In the end, however, I felt rather privileged that someone had been willing to go to so much unique trouble to provide me with such a truly Canadian experience.

PIERRE TRUDEAU WAS PRIME MINISTER when I moved to Canada in 1978. Justin Trudeau is prime minister as I write this. The year I arrived, Justin was just seven years old. Donald Trump is now president of the country where I was born. Donald Trump was a young lad of thirty-two, hard at work amassing his fortune, as I was moving north to get out of the rat race. The world moves forward in strange and mysterious ways.

Often I reflect on a young man's decision to go north when

many of his peers back in 1978 were going south (because it was warmer), or staying put in New York (because that was where the money was), or going west to California (because that was where the action was).

I reckon I went north to Nova Scotia, to Canada, because that was where the money *wasn't*, and because that was where the so-called action wasn't as well. And hey, I was young and tough, and so what if it was a little colder in the winter? Once I planted my flag in Canada, I knew this was where I was meant to be.

I like the benign patriotism we have. I like the kindness we show to refugees. I like the adventures and misadventures Canada has provided for me, the experiences that have helped shape who I am.

To that end, here comes a list. I know I am a Canadian because:

1. I have gone hiking and found myself hopelessly lost in a Northwest Territories wilderness with a veritable tornado of blackflies descending on me from above.
2. No one showed up to my poetry reading in Lloydminster, Saskatchewan, because Professional Outlaw Wrestling was in town that night.
3. I have surfed in Nova Scotia in January until the salt water froze on my forehead and my jaw muscles were so frozen I couldn't speak.
4. School kids on Vancouver Island once dared me to kiss a twenty-five-centimetre–long banana slug on the forest floor near Tofino—and I did.
5. During a February blizzard, I walked down a rural country road with my kids tied to a rope so they wouldn't blow away.

6. School kids all across Newfoundland have addressed me as "Sir"—except for the one feisty lad who preferred to address me as "Shaggy."

7. I've raced the tides of Fundy across a muddy sea floor with water lapping at my feet and my shoes sucking red mud with every step.

8. I've holed up alone in a motel room in Sudbury, Ontario, one dark and stormy night, feeling like the loneliest person on the planet.

9. I've watched a man in Happy Valley, Labrador, try to bring on spring by using a lawnmower to break up the deep snow in his front yard in May.

10. I've sat in the Saskatoon bus terminal at eight o'clock on a Sunday morning watching old grizzled men eat toast and bacon while I wrote a poem.

11. I've dutifully carried an umbrella over my head on a perfectly clear morning in Banff to bluff a posse of elk into thinking I was bigger than them.

12. I've woken up near the shores of the Strait of Belle Isle with a bear in my bedroom.

So, on this, my thirty-ninth year in this northern land, I reflect on these and many more images of your multifaceted self, Canada.

Thanks for the memories. And have a good one, eh?

Sincerely,
Lesley Choyce
Lawrencetown Beach, Canada
July 1, 2017

SHORT ATTENTION SPANS IN THE LAND OF THE ZOMBIES

I N 1980, THE AMERICAN AUTHOR MAGGIE JACKSON WROTE, IN HER book *Distracted: The Erosion of Attention and the Coming Dark Age*: "The way we live is eroding our capacity for deep, sustained, perceptive attention." She had fears that, because of all the distractions in our lives, we were losing our ability for sustained thought. She concluded that "an epidemic erosion of attention is a sure sign of an impending dark age."

Yes, a dark age. What do you think about that?

The official Dark Ages was a time in Europe from the fall of the Western Roman Empire in the fifth century to the time of the Renaissance in the fifteenth century. I doubt it could have been completely "dark" for so many centuries, but some historians consider it a time of repression, ignorance, and superstition, during which bigots and tyrants ruled many countries. The poet Petrarch, in the fourteenth century, viewed his time as a dismal one, writing: "This sleep of forgetfulness will not last for ever. When the darkness has been dispersed, our descendants can come again in the former pure radiance."

Well, it's now 2017, and because of all the distractions and erosion of thinking in the last thirty-seven years, we may have already entered some sort of neo-medieval Dark Age. The trouble is that we're caught up in so many arresting, trivial digital diversions that we don't have the ability to perceive what's happened.

Not me, of course. I've been paying attention. Or at least I think I have.

Okay, okay. We're probably all having too much fun texting and blogging and watching downloaded movies, tweeting and Instagramming and finding new and clever apps that fill our short little attention spans to even care about what we've lost. But humour me, for a bit, just in case there is something here of significance.

What exactly is sustained thought and why is it so important? (Have I lost you yet?) As the words suggest, sustained thought is sitting quietly somewhere (if such quiet can be found in our mega-info-muddled universe) and thinking about a thing for an extended period of time. In the old days, this was how we solved problems. Maybe it was just one person or a group of people, sitting together without distractions, seeking solutions to a real dilemma like how to stop Hitler or how to put a man on the moon or how to figure out why there is a hole in the ozone layer.

Certainly, there are a relative few among us ensconced in rarefied professions—think tanks—who are tackling monumental problems on everyone's behalf. But most of us simply race on into our futures without taking much time to sit and ponder at all.

If you don't use it, you lose it, as the saying goes. And if Jackson was even the slightest bit correct back in the rather staid, tame, and technologically challenged 1980s, it may already be too late.

When was the last time you sat quietly somewhere and did nothing but think? I like to believe it is what we occasionally did in the days before the avalanche of information and technology. If you were trying to solve a problem—personal, political, or global—you sat down and thought long and hard about it. Your mind was a tool you used to work things out. It required quiet and focus. And, for many, this tool worked very well.

Author Wilfred Arlan Peterson, in *The Art of Living, Day by Day: Three Hundred and Sixty-five Thoughts, Ideas, Ideals, Experiences, Adventures, Inspirations, to Enrich Your Life,* said this about sustained thought: "As a single footstep will not make a path on the earth, so a single thought will not make a pathway in the mind. To make a deep physical path, we walk again and again. To make a deep mental path, we must think over and over the kind of thoughts we wish to dominate our lives."

I was baffled a number of years ago when zombies suddenly became all the rage in books and movies and on TV. I had always thought of zombies as a product of bad 1950s and 1960s science fiction movies. But there they were, bursting back onto the pop culture scene with a vengeance, and even today these drooling, mindless living-dead icons are alive and well in mass media. There seems to be no stopping them.

As a card-carrying Luddite—a man who owns an old flip-style cellphone but rarely turns it on—I've detected, over the last decade or so, a change that perplexes and bothers me. Once upon a time, I could walk across the Dalhousie University campus and former students would see me, smile, say hello, and maybe even stop to chat about the weather or a Walt Whitman poem. But as cellphones became ubiquitous, students stopped saying hello, and they never stopped to chat about free verse anymore. Instead, between classes, it seemed imperative that they talk on their cell-phones to, well, probably other students somewhere on campus on their cellphones. Their eyes were always down as they walked along.

I used to see clusters of students, all on their cellphones, talking to people who were not there with them. I did not fully recognize this at the time, but it was perhaps the first step toward the looming zombie nation. Cellphone conversations were soon replaced with texting, and I began to observe the phenomenon of what I called cluster-texting along University Avenue. Walking and texting, too, became the fashion. Heads down, thumbs wig-gling away on screens, and a reckless lack of regard for others sharing the sidewalk.

Where once students smiled, made eye contact, and said hello, they now breeze on by, zoned out like the zombies they watch on Netflix. It is common now for me to have to step off the sidewalk onto someone's lawn so I don't get knocked over by someone walking and texting. Zombie nation has arrived.

I've been counselled that I should just roll with the times: get the latest iPhone and load up on apps, re-open my Facebook account, move up to Instagram, follow world leaders on Twitter, and, with my head down and focussed on a two-inch by three-inch screen, blithely waltz into the future.

To paraphrase Neil Young, however, "I've seen the iPhone and the damage done."

It's sometimes a battle to convince students to turn off their phones in class, to ignore text messages—to actually be there in the present, in class or elsewhere. I've seen more than one student of mine throw away their university education because they were truly addicted to Facebook. They were so heavily embedded in their virtual world of friends that they did not attend class, fearing they would miss something happening online. Video games, too, have taken their toll.

It gets harder and harder to sustain thought in the real world while the virtual world beckons with an endless cascade of new and enticing information to be tapped into, streamed, downloaded, retweeted, and regurgitated.

Back in the 1980s, Maggie Jackson despaired at the fifty million websites, seventy-five million blogs, and other "snowstorms of information" that would distract us and prevent sustained thought. (If I were a more ambitious researcher, I would try to update those statistics but I won't. It would scare the hell out of me—and make me more worried.)

Suffice it to say, we are over-informed with the trite and trivial and are becoming more and more under-informed about the really important things. With shorter and shorter attention spans brought on by byte-sized and mini-byte-sized trinkets of information, we may actually lose our capacity to think long and hard about our lives and the important issues that affect us. Easy, often inaccurate, information, and seductive, silly images, along with instant communication with hundreds of erstwhile friends, continue to lure us away from our own deep thoughts.

Timothy Leary once advised my generation to turn on, tune in, and drop out. My message to the contemporary world today, ladies and gentlemen, is to turn in, tune out, and drop your latest communication device into the nearest electronics recycling bin.

WATER FROM THE WELL

A FEW YEARS BACK I FELL THROUGH THE FLAT ROOF OVER MY backyard well. The event was long overdue, since I knew the wood was rotten but I had chosen to ignore the problem. Although it came as a bit of a shock, I was glad it was me who had fallen through and not someone else.

I had dug this well on the old property more than thirty years before and it had been a task filled with equal amounts of joy and frustration. There was a lot of cursing and some well-earned blisters but, in the end, I was proud of my accomplishment.

The year was 1979 and my yearly income was roughly $2,000. I had purchased on old farmhouse near the beach for $14,900. It didn't have running water, but it was perched on a soggy hill, and there was a small stream running through the dirt-floor basement. I had a good inkling that all I had to do was start digging behind the house and I'd strike water.

Having grown up in a place with sandy soil where I had dug many forts, I was sure a shovel would do the trick. That was, until I discovered there are more than a few rocks wherever a person might care to dig in this fair province. The handle on my shovel broke on the first sizable stone I attempted to dislodge from the soil.

I had an old pickaxe that had once belonged to my grand-father, so I enlisted that for the big dig. It defeated some small chunks of slate and shale, but seemed inadequate for the harder and larger stones it confronted. I tried not to become discouraged.

You must keep in mind that I began this project with much enthusiasm. I had, after all, chosen to move back to the land—a noble thing at any time and in any place. With poet and philopso-pher Henry David Thoreau in mind, I was hoping to be somewhat self-sufficient and as little dependent on the civilized world as possible. I was very idealistic and optimistic in those days—what I believed to be a winning combination—and all I was doing was digging a hole in the ground. How difficult could that be?

It turned out to be very difficult, indeed. My grandpop's pickaxe and I were up against rocks the size of basketballs and toaster ovens and TV sets. I borrowed a pry bar from a neigh-bour; I pried as I pleaded with the gods of the firmament, and I made slow-but-steady headway. After a week or so I had a cre-ated a knee-deep muddy hole and was sloshing around in there in my rubber boots as I pondered next steps and new geological adversaries.

Along the way, I marvelled at the various rectangular chunks of shiny stuff embedded in the slate that appeared to be…well, gold. I collected them in an old coffee can, washed them up, and was starting to suspect that my well may have been filled with wealth as well as muddy water. I pondered the irony of the fact that, living here in an old farmhouse, having forsaken the comfort of suburban life and consumerism, I may well have become rich, wrecking my dreams of idealistic self-imposed poverty.

I decided not to tell anyone about the gold, lest someone buy up the mineral rights to my beloved estate and start gouging at the land with massive machinery. It didn't take much research (in those days, one actually went to a library, though) to realize I had subsoils studded with iron pyrite—the proverbial gold of fools—and that pleased me about as much as anything could.

In order to speed up the excavation, I hired some local teenagers to help me dig. It came as no surprise that they lasted only a few hours each before bowing out of the well-digging business. They and many others offered advice concerning backhoes and drilling machines, but I would have none of it.

After about a month, I had what I considered a bit of bad luck: I hit bedrock. Not just another big stone, but the real deal. I was only seven feet down, but clearly it was the end of the line. The good news was that there seemed to be plenty of water.

My next task was to use some of the rocks I'd taken out of the well to create a cylindrical wall around my pool of dirty water. I had studied other rural wells and was much impressed by the handiwork of the old-timers. I did a pretty poor job of it, but in the end I had walls and, yes, a well.

I built a flat platform atop my rock well walls and, when I was finished, I stood upon it with pride, beaming into the morning sun with a cup of coffee in my hand. The water cleared up after a while and I installed a hand pump—another small step for this man as he slowly proceeded to catch up with the technology of the current century.

YEARS LATER, ON A RAW March day, I was standing there on those rotten boards above my well, admiring the spruce trees on the back hill. I heard a loud crack and then I dropped through, catching myself with my elbows on the unbroken boards with my legs dangling below, my feet kicking at the water. I didn't get hurt, but I felt a sense of wonder about the things that catch us off guard, the things that shock and surprise us when we are least expecting them.

You may think it's odd, but I hung there for a bit, contemplating my situation. If someone had arrived just then, they would have seen the top third of a sixty-year-old man propped up on his elbows while the rest of him dangled below the well cover. I think I actually had a smile on my face, which would have confirmed to the observer that I was probably a lunatic.

You may not be shocked to know I have moved on to cleaner and ever-more civilized water for consumption, employing not only a deep drilled well, but conditioners, reverse osmosis filters, and a refrigerator that makes ice cubes without me lifting a finger. Like other Canadians, I feel lucky we have such an abundance of everything—including water.

I ponder my old well today, though, because I read recently that 650 million people in the world live without safe water and 315 million children die each year from water-related illnesses. Lack of water is one of the crucial factors that drives people to leave sub-Saharan Africa and seek refuge elsewhere.

Canada has, within its borders, over 20 percent of the world's fresh water supply, although much of that is locked up underground or in glaciers. Naturally, the Americans would like a stake in our water wealth, but that probably would not help the water-deprived people of Africa, India, or anywhere else, and it's unlikely that we will be towing many icebergs to countries like Libya, Sudan, or Ethiopia.

Maybe my well-digging days are not over. I have a new shovel, and I still have my grandfather's pickaxe, but if I'm being honest, I'm probably not about to set off for Africa to dig holes. Instead, I think I'll do what I can do from here—dig deep into my pockets and find some money to donate to the worthy water charities that are doing good work around the world.

JIMMY BUFFETT STOLE MY WETSUIT BOOTS

IT'S BEEN OVER SEVEN YEARS NOW, AND I GUESS YOU COULD SAY I'm holding a grudge—but this story is true. When I woke up on the morning of September 20, 2010, my wetsuit boots were gone, and although I probably could not prove it in a court of law, I am dead certain that Jimmy Buffett, Mr. Margaritaville himself, stole them.

You are probably scratching your head in disbelief, wondering how such a heinous crime could come to pass on the otherwise bucolic Eastern Shore of Nova Scotia. And therein lies the tale.

I had been home minding my own business when singer-songwriter Lennie Gallant phoned to say a friend of his who had recorded one of his songs was coming to Nova Scotia, and he wanted to go surfing. Turns out said friend was Jimmy Buffett, and Lennie wondered if I would take Jimmy and his buddy John out for a late-afternoon surf session at the point at Lawrencetown.

It seemed like the right thing to do at the time. I said "Sure!" and offered to have a celebratory kitchen party at my two-hundred-year-old farmhouse by the beach afterward. I was psyched that it was shaping up to be a memorable evening. Jimmy himself called me from his cellphone a couple of times that afternoon as he headed up the coast. He was looking for a surf report and I was happy to say I thought we'd have some fairly decent four-foot walls without too much chop by the time he got here.

Late that afternoon, Jimmy and his friend arrived at my place. He was driving a bright lime green top-of-the-line camping van (which they'd named, appropriately, "Lime Green") with surfboards strapped to the sides. He didn't look anything like the Jimmy Buffett I remembered from his early days of success, but then most of us over sixty don't quite have the same hair or pretty-boy faces we had when we were singing folk songs in the 1970s, nor do we necessarily fit into the same wetsuits we once wore as wannabe surfers. Nonetheless, Jimmy had a grand smile and a firm handshake and, as expected, he seemed like a fun guy to surf and hang out with.

He and his buddy had driven Lime Green north from his home on Long Island. I couldn't quite picture a rock pirate like him living in the suburbs of New York City, a place I had gladly escaped in order to find refuge in Nova Scotia. But stranger things have happened, I suppose.

His van, he told me with great pride, had undergone a conversion so it could run on fuels other than gasoline. I heartily congratulated him on such an environmentally friendly move. "Yep," he said proudly. "We mostly burn discarded cooking oil from restaurants that would usually be thrown away. We have depots for such things in the States." He went on to say he was having a hard time locating a good supply of the stuff in Nova Scotia. "Old oil from a french-fryer will do the trick. It doesn't even matter if it's rancid," he said, taking off his signature sunglasses and staring up into the wispy fog that half-hid the sun.

I said I'd call around and see if I could come up with thirty or so gallons of rancid vegetable oil; he appreciated that, patting me on the back like we were old chums.

His van drew considerable attention as we pulled into the parking lot near the point at Lawrencetown. The water was fairly crowded for Nova Scotia, but we slipped into our wetsuits and boots (no gloves) and paddled out to the lineup. Only one of my surfing buddies, a Buffett fan (a "Parrot Head," as they sometimes call themselves) recognized Jimmy and said hi. Most of the other surfers ignored him. Jimmy did get some dirty looks from a few local guys as he paddled into more than his fair share of waves. New York surfers, you have to understand, are a fair shake more aggressive in the water than Nova Scotian surfers, so I say this with all due respect.

It turned out to be a fun surf session all around. Jim and his buddy were stoked, and Jimmy kept saying things like, "It's great that an old fart like me can still catch a few waves with the boys." Born and raised in Mississippi and Alabama, he had maintained a stylish southern drawl that had served him well on stage over the years, and as he spoke it brought back memories of my own days surfing in the southern US.

After maybe an hour and a half, the sun began to set as we paddled ashore and headed back to my house for dinner and music. Once there, we all threw our wetsuit gear out on the wooden picnic table on the hillside to drip for the night, then headed indoors to avoid the mosquitoes.

Lennie had graciously prepared lobster and scallops for us in my kitchen and I told Jimmy he should eat, settle in, and stay the night in our empty bedroom. He smiled that signature smile and said, "Much obliged."

After the feast, we enjoyed an outstanding evening of Jimmy and Lennie trading tunes on their guitars in my old kitchen and listening to Jimmy's tales of his life on the road. A reviewer for *The Cleveland Plain Dealer* once said of one of Jimmy's books: "Buffett is the literary version of the best barstool buddy you ever ran into." Later, when I checked out some YouTube footage of Buffett's concerts, it became clear that the persona of the Jimmy Buffett in my kitchen was pretty much the same as the Jimmy Buffett on stage in front of thousands. I guess you have to have some respect for someone who has that kind of authenticity, onstage and off.

When we were asked if we wanted to hear any favourite songs, none of us present were foolish enough to ask him to play "Margaritaville" but I did persuade him to play a lesser-known early tune of his called "Come Monday," a bittersweet melodic ballad that tugs at the heartstrings.

It turned into a late night, and my wife, joking she might not get up early enough to arrive in time for her job as a high school principal, asked Jimmy to write her a note excusing her tardiness. Pen in hand, Jimmy wrote:

> *To whom it may concern,*
>
> *Please excuse Principal Choyce for not arriving on time today. I take full responsibility for her tardiness.*
>
> *Sincerely,*
> *Jimmy Buffett*

Jimmy thanked us and said he and John needed to get some shut-eye. They wanted to be up quite early in the morning, probably while it was still dark, to drive to the airport. His private plane was being flown up from New York and his pilot would drive Lime Green back to New York, provided they could find enough old french fry oil. Jimmy, a long-time pilot, would fly himself home, saving some time because he had a concert in Paris to get to.

The visitors slept in my now–grown-up daughters' bedrooms amidst posters of unicorns, *Star Trek,* and *Beverly Hills 90210.*

By the time Linda and I got up in the morning, Lime Green and the New York surfers were long gone. There was, however, incriminating evidence that a genuine Maritime kitchen party had taken place. Note in hand, Linda headed off to work, but stopped as she was walking down the driveway when she heard my gasp of despair. I had gone outside to retrieve my wetsuit and discovered my sixty-dollar wetsuit boots were missing.

I checked my car and looked around on the grass, but soon realized they were gone. For reasons that still confound me to this day, I can only assume that when Mr. Margaritaville rose before dawn and collected his surfing gear, he grabbed my wetsuit boots and spirited them away with his own gear.

I know what you are thinking: it was probably just an accident. And perhaps that is what his fans would say in his defense. A busy rock/country music star in a rush to get to a concert in Paris is likely to unwittingly grab the damp wetsuit boots of his host, a mild-mannered Nova Scotian surfer and poet. This could be true.

But, as the days passed, I kept hoping Jimmy would take stock of his surfing gear and discover a pair of neoprene boots that did not fit his Mississippi feet. And upon such a discovery, Mr.

Buffett would realize the crime (accidental or otherwise). At such time, one would assume, Mr. Buffett would email an apology and, if his heart was in the right place, send those boots (or possibly a newer, state-of-the-art pair) northward to the Choyce residence.

Alas, this busy, globetrotting singer (and restaurant-chain mogul, too, I might add) had moved on to bright stages and more exotic surfing destinations. I guess I'll never learn the full truth about those boots. In order to purge the damage to my soul, I did attempt to write a country song called "Jimmy Buffett Stole My Wetsuit Boots." It wasn't the best song I ever wrote, but I was hoping that if it became a hit, I might hear from other surfers in various parts of the world who'd had a similar experience when Jimmy Buffett was in town.

BUYING MY TWENTY-THIRD CAR

IREMEMBER EVERY CAR I'VE EVER BOUGHT AND, AS FAR AS I CAN calculate, the total number of automobiles I have owned is twenty-three. I've never purchased a brand new car and I don't really have a desire to do so; a used vehicle is just fine for me. I get a car dirty pretty quickly, hauling around my surfboard, sitting behind the wheel in a sea-soaked wetsuit, chauffeuring my dog to the beach, and sometimes hauling class-A gravel in the trunk for my driveway.

I recall carting seaweed for my garden from Three Fathom Harbour in the back of an old Ford Escort station wagon, and little hopping insects would commute to Halifax with me for several days afterward. The car would also smell pretty bad. I remember many years ago bringing seaweed from the beach in the spring, and then going to the airport to pick up Cape Breton/Hollywood moviemaker Daniel Petrie Sr., who had directed films like *Fort Apache, The Bronx,* and *The Bay Boy.* I had to apologize profusely for the little bugs and the smelly car, but being a polite Cape Bretoner, Dan said he didn't notice the smell.

Even now, I still occasionally gather up seaweed in the spring to fertilize my garden—which is why it would be pointless to buy a brand new vehicle.

For my twenty-third automobile, I ended up at a local dealer of pre-owned vehicles, where I had a friendly salesman who did his job well. He was likeable, and told me no more and no less than what I asked about the car. I pretty much knew what I wanted and how much I could spend. I liked the car so I sold myself on it.

I traded in my old car—always an emotional moment for me. I have honestly shed a tear over many a hunk of rusting metal— cars that have safely carried me home on treacherous black-ice roads; cars that have not run out of gas when they should have; cars that have dutifully transported my kids to school on rainy mornings. Cars that have been part of my everyday life. Some people may think a car is just an object, a thing, but I have a notion that we imbue them with some of our own spirit. They will always be automotive, but the owner invests some of himself or herself in the car they drive, so when we sell them or drop them off at the junkyard, we lose a little of ourselves. This is because the car has history—it has been part of the family. "I'm sorry," I want to say. "Thanks for being good to us. I wish you well. So long."

Once you have a new car, you need to get used to its unusual, more modern ways: automatic windshield wipers that go on of their own accord when it rains, back-up video cameras, all manner of buttons on the steering wheel. (Was it really that hard to reach a finger out to the dashboard and push a button to change a radio station?) And is it just me, or does anyone else miss windows that you rolled down manually? Was it really that much physical effort? A winter or two ago, the electric window mechanism on Linda's car broke while I was driving with the window down, which elicited considerable blasphemy from me because we were driving in a blizzard across the A. Murray MacKay Bridge.

My 2008 Kia Rondo had a different, but equally annoying,

problem. The electric locking mechanism on the rear right door broke, leaving the door permanently locked. (It would have cost over five hundred dollars, I was told by the dealer, to have it fixed.) I stubbornly refused, for several years, to pay to have it fixed, but the problem solved itself when I traded the car in on my latest set of wheels.

So I'm an advocate for fewer electric features in our cars and more manual controls. Sadly, the latest automotive news suggests that such practical improvements are not in the offing. Instead, in the not-so-distant future, my car will be driving me. Based on my experiences with electric windows, locks, and supposedly artificially intelligent windshield wipers, I remain a sceptic.

But buying the twenty-third car in my short lifetime prompted me to reminisce about some of the mechanical beasts of burden I have owned down through the years. And since I've realized that such musings have no place in long-winded yarns at social gatherings, I thought I could drive down memory lane by writing this—but I promise to just hit the high notes, and spare you the protracted version.

I PURCHASED MY FIRST CAR with the money I'd earned delivering newspapers on my bicycle. It was a 1957 Chevy station wagon. The year was 1967 and I was sixteen years old. There were cigarette burns in the front seat (so common in those days) and my mother made me a new seat-cover out of black velour. I didn't have a license, so I drove that beauty around our rather small backyard, eventually denting the front fender on a black locust tree. I punched the dent out myself (and, eventually, I passed my driver's test). That wagon was a "surfmobile" and a loyal friend, as only your first car can be—right up until it was stolen one night while I was in a movie theatre watching Stanley Kubrick's *2001: A Space Odyssey*.

I was carless briefly, until I spotted a 1959 Nash Metropolitan rusting away in a neighbour's backyard. I have no idea why that ridiculous little car, one of the first true compact cars in North America, caught my fancy. It could have been that the price was right: fifty dollars, if I could tow it away, which I did with the help of my brother and father.

The car was two-toned: pink and white. It was the complete opposite of what any level-headed teenaged male would want to be seen driving in. It had a miniscule Austin-Healey engine, which my brother got running after putting in a new head gasket. The gearshift stuck out of the dashboard, since there was so little room for anything in the car. It shifted in a clockwise circle. There wasn't any legitimate room for a person in the back seat (barely room for groceries, really), but all the seats folded down and the divider between the diminutive trunk and the rest of the car folded down as well. This allowed me to sleep fully prone while on road trips to the shore, or to Woodstock, or wherever I ended up on my travels.

My next car was a 1962 Ford Galaxie convertible. I had never wanted a convertible, and I still have no idea why anyone would want one. But, again, the price was right and my hair was long, so I must have thought I looked cool letting my locks stream in the wind as I tooled around the suburbs. This one took me back and forth to university in North Carolina for a few years until I realized it leaked a bit of oil, consumed a lot of gas, and didn't quite have the right political look about it for a radically inclined guy like me.

I gave up the Galaxie in 1972 and bought the first in a string of Volkswagens. I had a '59, a '62, and a '65 Beetle, all in a row.

Two were black and one was a hand-painted green, with a patina of rust on both the hood and the rear. Little did I know at the time that the car had been Hitler's idea as he had encouraged Ferdinand Porsche to create a "people's car" way back in 1935. How odd that such a creation would become popular in North America, especially among those in the counterculture in the early 1970s.

What I remember most about the Bugs was their heating system. The car's designers had figured out a way to have the air that flowed underneath the air-cooled engine (which was in the rear of the car) pumped into the little cabin. Once the engines started leaking oil and exhaust, that air carried the oil and exhaust fumes directly into the car.

Undaunted by such concerns, I moved up a notch in the German automotive world by purchasing a Volkswagen van. Once again, oddly, this one turned out to be pink and white, and had a canvas top that opened—a kind of van/convertible. My brother had some green paint left over from my Beetle, so this ended up green as well. It was much more comfortable to sleep in than my Nash Metropolitan had been, and it proved most useful for hauling firewood and for commandeering items found in the trash—including a mahogany console combination-television-and-stereo set.

I won't try to fill in all the automobiles I had from 1975 to 2016. That would fill a book, and it would undoubtedly be a book that no one would want to read. But in 1978, when I moved to Nova Scotia, I crossed the border into St. Stephen, New Brunswick, in a 1968 Ford Econoline van. My brother Gordy had turned it into a camper for me and had painted it brown—this time, with an air gun. (He used the same batch of paint to restore my old rusty refrigerator at the same time.) In the Econoline I had a sink, a bed, and a Coleman stove. I could have lived in it if I'd had to.

In the move to Canada, I brought that brown refrigerator, an old Rototiller that my dad had given me, and as much stuff as I thought I could truck here to begin a new life as a Nova Scotian. The van only lasted a few years, however—Nova Scotia winters being what they are. But I was sad to sell it and I shed at least one more tear as I watched it being driven away.

I guess I was never loyal to any single brand of automobile, because there have been Toyotas, Fords, Chevrolets, Datsuns, Pontiacs, Dodges, and even a bright yellow Škoda in my automotive history. Most would have eventually ended up in junkyards and sold for scrap. Undoubtedly, their little metallic molecules, in one form or another, are probably spread all over the planet. It's a little bit like reincarnation, if you think about it. I doubt cars have the same kinds of souls as humans, but I still have that notion they carry a little of the driver's spirit in those molecules while you own them. And maybe some of that spirit goes with them into their next incarnation. Perhaps some of the steel of my old '57 Chevy is now part of a lawn chair at a posh hotel in Singapore or in the spokes of a bicycle in South Africa.

That's what I'm hoping, anyway.

THE DEATH OF TELEVISION AND OTHER GOOD NEWS

TELEVISION IS DEAD, LONG LIVE TELEVISION. OR SOMETHING like that.

Once upon a time, I spent a large part of every evening watching television shows I really didn't want to watch. In other words, I watched what was available. Exactly why I did this, I'm not sure. But I was not alone. Mind-numbing sitcoms abounded on TV, and still do...but I don't watch them anymore.

Each new fall season seemed to bring worse shows to the networks. I thought things couldn't possibly get any worse until the emergence of so-called reality TV. The decline was fast and steady from there. Even when I had satellite TV, it would take considerable time to scan the heavens to find anything at all stimulating to the mind. Sometimes I found myself watching international stations from Portugal and even Russia just to see if other countries had better programming than North America. Alas, they did not.

In my travels, I also discovered how banal British TV can be, how melodramatically absurd Italian dramas are, and how tedious Icelandic news broadcasts can be. Undoubtedly, some of the worst TV I've ever seen was in Austria—especially the traditional music shows. But no nation spends more money producing—and more time watching—drivel than America, and, of course, we end up watching what they watch.

Let me reminisce about TV in Nova Scotia in the early-to-mid-1980s. As I recall, I could pick up two stations with my rabbit-ears antenna: CBC and CTV. Reception was poor out here in the sticks but it was all we had, and I appreciated the local content.

I remember music shows like *Up Home Tonight*, and I was truly stoked by the musicians Gordon Stobbe hosted on the show. John Allan Cameron had a series on CBC-TV that was a blast. *Land and Sea* was good because the content was about subjects that were of interest to me. David Suzuki came along and was so impassioned about saving the planet on *The Nature of Things* that I was enthralled. I can also remember Murray McLaughlin doing a special called *Floating Over Canada* in which he flew a small plane across the country, and I kept thinking what a wonderfully big, woodsy, underpopulated land this was, and how lucky I was to be living here.

I'd stay up late to watch Frank Cameron walk us through the news of the day. He often looked a bit tired, and I wondered if the Mother Corp was overworking him and if that was taking a toll on his health. But Frank's still kicking, so I guess the work didn't do him too much harm.

Whenever my relatives from the States came to visit, they were amazed at how little crime there was in Nova Scotia—and that the robbing of a candy store in Truro could end up as a lead story on the nightly TV newscast. I thought the news reports about rug-hooking in Chéticamp and chainsaw carvers in Queens County were just great.

I was reminded recently of the "professional" wrestling matches on regional TV in those days. I was not a fan of Atlantic Grand Prix Wrestling at the time, but compared to what is offered up as sport these days on the tube, that was just good, clean fun. Gone but not forgotten are the matches of Emile Duprée, Killer Karl Krupp, and The Great Malumba.

In the midst of the steady decline of television entertainment, oddly enough, I was persuaded to host my own television show. I had a slot on Channel 10 (the local cable access channel) interviewing authors on a head-and-shoulders interview show called *East Coast Authors*; it lasted for nearly a decade. On the studio set, I would sit down with an author and ask what I thought were interesting questions, and my guest would answer in a most intelligent and interesting fashion. It sounds pretty unexciting, I admit, but I garnered a small but loyal (at least in my mind) audience. We didn't have much, but we had something missing from a lot of commercial TV: content. Real people—with real ideas and experiences—who had written books.

East Coast Authors evolved into *Choyce Words*, which was picked up by PBS in Maine and then bumped from Eastlink; a new version of it aired on VisionTV, and later on the BookTelevision channel as *Off the Page*. My so-called TV career lasted for more than three hundred shows until BookTelevision bumped the show in favour of endless reruns of *Little House on the Prairie* and *Xena: Warrior Princess*.

While we were still on the air somebody actually tried to figure out our demographic, and it was determined that our audience was mostly women over sixty. This was my fan base. Men, of course, were watching *Hockey Night in Canada* and NFL football. But the older female demographic helped to explain why there were so many beauty products and denture commercials intruding on my literary conversations.

I had other forays into more traditional commercial television: I was interviewed on *The Vicki Gabereau Show* in Vancouver; I conversed with author Judy Blume about teen fiction on another national TV talk show. But I was reminded of the harsh realities of TV entertainment when I flew to Toronto on a book tour, scheduled to be on CTV's morning newsmagazine program, *Canada AM,* only to be bumped at the very last minute when the producer told me they would instead be interviewing a British author named Andrew Morton who had just come to town to promote his book about Princess Diana. (This chapter seems to be filled with my grudges and gripes about a medium that has had, whether I like it or not, a fairly profound influence on our lives and culture).

A few years ago I severed the cable between me and the broadcasting gods who brought entertainment to the big-screen TV in my living room. Aside from *60 Minutes* and the odd *Seinfeld* rerun, I can't say I miss traditional television one iota. Here in the household, Linda and I do watch a lot of movies—mostly good ones, as well as a few clunkers.

We've discovered that many of the TV series' airing on Netflix are relentlessly dark and cheerless. From *Breaking Bad* to *Damages* to *Narcos,* I've had my fill of greed, lust, and sheer meanness after a couple of episodes. Don't even get me going about *Making a Murderer.*

I am well aware that the current options for entertainment via YouTube, Netflix, and all the rest are virtually endless. I am sure I will hone my skills at finding the good stuff amongst the malarkey and claptrap. It's just that there's something mildly depressing about sitting before a TV screen toggling away at a remote and discovering the avalanche of entertainment mediocrity available. If Marshall McLuhan was still with us, he could probably explain with precision the nature of the damage it is doing to my brain, if not my soul.

At such moments, when the despair settles over me like a damp, insidious fog, I seek out the inner courage it takes to simply turn off the electronic beast entirely, take a deep breath, and do what any sane man would do in such a moment: settle his glasses snugly upon his nose and reach over for a really good book.

FEUDING WITH THE FASHIONISTAS

I COULDN'T HELP BUT NOTICE THAT SHREDDED PANTS ARE BACK IN style. Apparently, they are officially known as distressed jeans. You can even watch YouTube videos to learn how to create DIY distressed jeans. As a twelve-year-old boy wandering fields and forests, I was, apparently, way ahead of my time, ripping my own jeans on fences, thorns, barbed wire, and tree branches. I had no idea that in my distant future, ripped-up pants would be sold at exorbitant prices to fashion-conscious men and women.

I could find no serious consumer research regarding the phenomenon, but there's plenty of propaganda on the internet from fashionistas—those overly ambitious promoters, designers, and fans of the latest fashions. In my search, I allowed Google to steer me toward clothing websites offering up many, many options for women's and men's shredded pants. I discovered that you could purchase something called "Women's 7 For All Mankind Ripped High Waist Skinny Jeans." The price was $229. The pants were touted as having "shredded holes and whiskering perfect for the time-worn look of figure-hugging skinnies that go with just about everything in your closet"—whatever that sentence means.

Well, not my closet. Seeking respite from the shredding, I took a quick trip to the Eddie Bauer site and was assured that

Eddie was having nothing to do with this phenomenon. Pants are pants—you don't want to go hiking or mountain climbing in pants that are already ripped. That layer of denim is there to protect your knees, calves, and ankles from damage. But, on the other hand, if you are tempted to pop onto the Saks Fifth Avenue website, they too will most happily sell you jeans with split knees or shredded thigh sections. In fact, in the wacky world of men's and women's clothing, you can get pants with any manner of whiskering, fraying, or tattering. You can find pants that have been slashed, slit, shredded, gashed, ruptured, or semi-crushed.

I say there's way too much violence in clothing these days.

For what it's worth, I wouldn't spend too much time worrying about your wardrobe if I were you. Fashion, in my book, is mostly a waste of time and money, but if you have a surplus of both, then fill your boots. Designers who come up with *new* (is that even possible?) fashion statements basically do one of three things: they promote a colour that's currently not in vogue—hot pink or lime green, for example; they "invent" something that is uniquely outrageous and downright silly; or they recycle something that came before that was uniquely outrageous and downright silly. So I don't have much spare change for fashion.

Architect and author Witold Rybczynski, in his book about the history of the screwdriver, *One Good Turn*, points out that the greatest of all fashion designers is an unknown person—undoubtedly a woman—who invented the button. When I told my students I was reading about the history of the screwdriver, one young man observed, "Man, you must have a lot of time on your hands." But I found the book fascinating, especially the aside about the button.

Rybczynski studied very old drawings and noticed that clothing consisted mainly of robes and sashes—stuff tied together—which I think is kind of cool and sexy, to be honest. But then, almost suddenly (as historical records go), artists started showing people wearing clothing with buttons. Buttons and buttonholes had to be invented more or less at the same time, of course. And the idea must have caught on big time.

I can hear the man of the house looking at his wife who is in the process of inventing the button, saying something like, "It will never work. The public will find it too complicated." Which it is, if you think about it. It requires a highly dexterous manipulation of a little round object—now plastic, but once upon a time made from bone or shell or hand-forged metals.

Many years after the button came the zipper, an invention I had been led to believe had been created by a Canadian. Alas, only recently I discovered through deeper research that the inventor was not, in fact, a Canadian. An American named Elias Howe had received a patent for something called an "Automatic, Continuous Clothing Closure" in 1851, but the public had not been much interested. In 1893 Whitcomb Judson displayed his "Clasp Locker" at the World's Fair, but again, the public gave it a yawn. Finally, Swedish-American Gideon Sundback came up with a much better version around 1913; he later joined a Canadian company that would manufacture what would become the modern zipper, so we can't entirely claim it as our own.

Metal zippers are quite functional, except on wetsuits, where they rust if you spend a lot of time in salt water like I do. But those plastic zippers with the really fine teeth are not to be trusted, especially on the fly of your pants. I learned this from personal experience during a public speaking debacle.

It happened like this: just before I had to give a lecture to a large auditorium of people, the zipper on the fly of my polyester pants split (I only wore polyester for a brief and misguided period of my life, so don't laugh too loudly). I had no suit jacket or sweater to pull down over the offending area, and had to borrow a safety pin from a woman who happened to have one in her purse. This half-convinced me that men should carry purses to keep tools and safety pins in—but this idea may not fly with everyone, I know. Men sometimes wear "fanny packs," although this always strikes me as something a person should only do while visiting Disney World or at Labour Day festivities.

It was a no-podium event so I spoke from behind my dinner plate at the head table. The safety pin only did half the job. I noticed people noticing, so I owned up to the problem mid-anecdote and used it as part of my little talk, which I believe was about how to be more creative in the workplace.

Stain-resistance is another fashion problem that needs to be addressed. I have a habit of spilling things on my clothing, so I prefer to wear dark clothing on which the coffee or spaghetti-sauce stains are not so obvious. Were I to start wearing white shirts, they would act as a kind of archive of my eating and drinking habits. A typical day might include a visual display of tea, egg, coffee, peanut butter, tofu (fortunately nearly invisible on a white shirt), mustard and/or ketchup, and possibly some cranberry juice made from the cranberries that grow on the hills of Lawrencetown.

I once interviewed American Beat writer and poet Allen Ginsberg on my TV show, and he wanted to talk about clothes, for some reason. He said he favoured the traditional "serviceable uniform" of blue jeans and a blue work shirt. Khaki was okay with him, too, as long as it wasn't military. Ginsberg was one of those thinkers, like Marshall McLuhan, who was right about 30 percent of the time with his iconoclastic ideas and predictions. But I think he was bang-on with this one.

Jeans or "dungarees," as we used to call them as kids, are indeed an excellent clothing option. You can work in the garden with them or you can wear them to church. You'd think I would approve of the ones with buttons on the crotches, but I don't. Too much wrestling. I also think the more basic the pair of jeans the better. However, I feel it's necessary to avoid any pair of jeans that appears to be making a fashion statement.

AFTER HAVING SAID SUCH HORRIBLE things about fashion, I'd still advise that it's worth it to wear clothes that make you feel and look good. I'd advise against wearing stuff that is too tight and cuts off the blood supply to any part of your anatomy, though. And while we're at it, I think men should probably abandon the whole ridiculous idea of suits and ties. Unfortunately, nowadays, whenever I see a man in a shiny suit, I think of Donald Trump. And most days, I'd prefer not to think of him at all.

If you want a new look, go to the second-hand clothing store and make a small investment in a new style. If your selection doesn't work, you can turf it back to the Salvation Army as a donation without losing much at all. I buy quite a few used T-shirts. I like having T-shirts with stuff written on them. "Surfers Against Apartheid" is in my T-shirt archive, as is "Shred Tough or Go Home to Momma." I also have a lot of T-shirts from places I never have been to and don't plan to visit in my lifetime.

But please, whatever you do, avoid spending your money on new clothes that flaunt the name of the company. I'm addicted to reading, so I will read any word put in front of me and it will stay in my mind while I'm driving or making soup (or sometimes doing both at the same time, with one of those little plug-in devices in my car). I would be thrilled to never see the name Tommy Hilfiger again. I rather long for the old days when, if you were going to put the name of your company on a sweatshirt, it would be in wavy, artsy, unreadable psychedelic script.

Which conjures up one final memory—paisley. I've saved all my old colourful swirly shirts and am waiting for the time that paisley will be back in fashion. Unless I missed a hiccup in the fashion world, paisley hasn't been in fashion since 1970, and it's just not fair. I blame the fashionistas.

PUPPY LOVE

WHEN OUR DOG, MURDO, DIED IN THE WINTER OF 2016, LINDA and I grieved as much as any dog owners have grieved over the loss of a long-time companion. For weeks, I continued to come home, expecting him to greet me at the door, only to suddenly remember that he was gone. Like any major loss, it took a while for it to fully sink in.

But as spring arrived, Linda and I agreed it was time to find another canine soul to share our home. Murdo had been a West Highland White Terrier and Linda was determined to get another Westie. And she wanted a puppy. In the past when it was time to find a family dog, I had always adopted whatever mutt came along, but this would be different. Much different.

For starters, I didn't know dogs could be expensive. I thought you simply located someone with an unwanted litter of puppies and they would be thrilled to give you one. Not so. After a search of the appropriate breeders in Nova Scotia, it turned out none would have a Westie puppy available anywhere in the province in the coming year. Linda suggested we might have to travel to New Brunswick or Newfoundland to find our dog. I said no way, no how. Who ever heard of having to drive to another province to get a dog?

Despite my rejection of such an idea, Linda surreptitiously persisted with her search. She found a breeder in Newfoundland who had Westie puppies for sale, but they were all taken. The woman in Newfoundland, however, said she knew of a friend in Ontario who would have a litter of puppies soon and, if we wanted, we could put in our order.

"Drive to Ontario for a dog?" I said. "Are you crazy?"

"Well, we could fly," Linda said.

"Fly somewhere to get a dog? Nobody does that."

Well, it turns out some people do—but we didn't. A road trip it would be, but not before Evelyn, the breeder in Ontario, thoroughly checked our credentials. Linda sent her the article I'd written for the *Chronicle Herald* about the death of Murdo, and that seemed to be the ticket.

In April we received a phone call from Evelyn letting us know the batch of puppies had come into the world and one was earmarked for us. We should show up in Reaboro, Ontario, in eight weeks. Now that I knew there was a puppy waiting for us, I decided a road trip to Ontario was not such a bad thing. But I still believed it would be a bit expensive just to bring home a dog, what with gas and meals and accommodation.

Somewhere along the line, my wife informed me that the dog itself would cost a sizable sum. We were, after all, not just adopting a dog but buying one. I'd never bought a dog before, so it came as a bit as a shock. The price tag was two thousand dollars.

By the time my fuzzy brain processed the amount, I realized it was already a done deal. So with travel, dog, designer dog food that the breeder insisted upon, various shots, and miscellaneous vet bills to come, even before we had our puppy, I was reminded that owning a dog is a serious investment of capital.

Eight weeks went by and finally we were on the road. I'd never driven through New Brunswick and Quebec in the summer, and it was a long but glorious ride: Halifax to Fredericton, Fredericton to Rivière-du-Loup, and up the St. Lawrence to Cornwall, Ontario, then on to Peterborough. Somewhere out there in rural Ontario a puppy was waiting for a home in a faraway province by the sea.

The day before meeting our new family member, I went into a pet store in Peterborough to purchase the designated dog food. "Really? It costs how much?" I asked the salesperson. *It's just dog food*, I wanted to say, but I was learning to keep my mouth shut about some things. Somehow, I couldn't get out of the store before I spotted a backpack designed for carrying a dog. It was pretty cool looking and had mesh covering in places, so the dog could breathe and, of course, look around as the person carrying the dog hiked.

I was thinking I could just buy a less expensive backpack at Canadian Tire and cut holes in it. But nevertheless, the backpack joined the dog-food bag in the car as we made the final leg of our journey to Reaboro. We arrived a bit early in the rural Ontario town, so we stopped at a small park. The grass was brown and it was hot. (Back in Nova Scotia, the grass was green and it was still cold.) I was feeling strangely not-at-home here in this inland province until I noticed the hiking trail running through the park. Checking out the sign, I discovered this was part of the Trans Canada Trail—the same hiking path that met the Atlantic Ocean at Lawrencetown Beach, my home.

Something about that discovery made me feel connected. As I sat on the dry grass and adjusted the straps on the doggie backpack, I had a vision of meeting our puppy, putting him in the backpack and heading east, hiking homeward step-by-step on the Trans Canada Trail until the salty spray of the North Atlantic kissed my lips. But I guess I decided it was just too long a walk.

KELTY (FULL NAME: KELTY MACGREGOR) was a little white fire-cracker of a dog. As my hiking vision quickly faded, we hit the road, more anxious than ever to introduce him to his new home.

We drove for seven straight hours and ended up just south of Quebec City at a motel that allowed pets (for an extra fee, of course). Naturally, Linda and I were woken up several times that night. Puppies have to pee at regular intervals, and that, of course, includes in the middle of the night. I began to realize raising a puppy was going to be a bit like raising a baby…and I hadn't done that for over thirty years.

Everywhere we stopped to walk the dog, people fussed over him. If Linda was not right there beside me, she would invariably return to find a strange woman talking to me and petting the dog. If you happen to be a single man out there, forget about online dating and go get yourself a Westie puppy. (You may have to take out a loan, however.)

But after driving for two long days, we were back in Nova Scotia with our new companion, who was peeing and pooping on the floor and making himself fully at home.

We started out trying to get the dog to sleep in a dog bed on the floor, but that didn't work. We tried to get him to sleep on a padded chair, pushed up against our bed, and that worked to some degree, but eventually Kelty would find his way onto our bed, curl up on one corner, then shift to another. Inevitably, he'd end up on my pillow, sleeping just above my head. It was a bit odd, but endearing, and I decided it was one of those things I could just get used to.

We hadn't finished spending money on him yet, though. One day we thought Kelty had a tooth infection and we took him to the vet, who told us he was only teething. That information, of course, was not free. Another time, Kelty ate a bee. The bee stung him hard on the roof of his mouth and he howled long and loud—and then he passed out. That scared the daylights out of us; I couldn't tell if he was breathing, so I gave him mouth-to-mouth resuscitation and we raced him back to the vet.

By the time we got there and explained the situation, Kelty was perfectly fine—breathing, alert, and looking again like a happy puppy.

Kelty has chewed and destroyed various items around our home—as any active young dog might. The list includes a brand new pair of my sandals, an assortment of socks, an exercise DVD, and a DVD of a movie called *Lions and Lambs*.

He's outgrown the backpack now, but I used to carry him around in it while I was shopping at the grocery store in Porters Lake. He would usually be quiet and most people wouldn't notice him, but as soon as he was spotted, a crowd would form and he would become the centre of attention.

He's house-trained now and rings a set of sleigh bells by the door when he wants to go out. His passion is walking on the beach, and most mornings he convinces us we should do just that before any other work gets done.

He grew despondent when he realized he was too big to crawl under the sofa anymore, but he consoled himself by continuing to curl up against my head in the middle of the night. I'm usually fast asleep, and he is so artful about it I don't usually realize he's there until I wake up in the morning.

I can't seem to stop him from chewing my pant leg, and he

has a small list of other faults Linda suggests are because "he's still a puppy." But he's coming up on his first birthday soon and I don't really want him to grow up and become just another adult dog.

On his really bad days, when I have to walk around the house peg-legged because I'm dragging a small white dog who has his teeth sunk into my pant leg, we refer to him as the West Highland terrorist. But usually he is a good dog. His life is filled with barking at the Arctic hares in the yard, watching for the appearance of dogs in Netflix movies—and there are plenty of dogs in the film business, it would appear—chasing balls, wind-blown seaweed, and seagulls on the beach, and feasting on dog food that is much pricier than the food I eat.

As dogs do, he teaches me things as we live our life with him. He knows how to live in the moment, how to live life to the fullest, and how to remain faithful to those he loves.

Recently we received our official "Purebred Dog Certificate of Registration" from the Canadian Kennel Club. It looks a lot like a university diploma and proclaims not only the dog's purebred status, but that he is the offspring of two well-documented parents whose official names are Perfect Wild Boy of Surprise and Forestfield Iremeberu. In the dog world, I guess, this is perhaps the equivalent to royalty.

But in the evening, as Kelty curls up by the fireplace with us, looking perfectly contented, I suspect he's not much different from those ancient dogs who first fell asleep by the fires of our ancestors, tens of thousands of years ago.

LUNCH AT THE LEFTOVER RESTAURANT

"WHAT'S YOUR FAVOURITE FOOD?"
For a long while now, I have answered that my favourite food is "leftovers." Think about it: you've had a hard day of work, you come home and you don't want to think about dinner, but you are so hungry you could eat a horse (not literally). You really don't want to cook, and you don't want to wait for a pizza delivery. And then you open the refrigerator and discover, to your immediate delight, that it's well-stocked with leftovers. Really good leftovers. And now you're a happy camper.

I'm guessing I am not alone in my passion (I hope that's not too strong a word) for leftovers. A quick check on Google for "leftover food recipes" lands a whopping 65,100,000 results. A lot of real and wannabe chefs are presumably out there offering advice on what to do with all your leftover chicken, cheese, and couscous.

Undoubtedly the best leftovers are from Christmas, Easter, and Thanksgiving Day dinners. Turkey leftovers from Thanksgiving will get you through two or three days before they start to lose their allure.

Some foods actually taste better the second time around. Homemade soups and stews are much better after a day or so.

I'm not that fond of cooking, and I don't really like dealing with the public, but, as a fiction writer and veteran daydreamer, I do a lot of what-if thinking. So, the other day, I came up with the (theoretical) idea of opening a posh niche dining venue called The Leftover Restaurant. It would serve only really good leftovers. Not food left on other people's plates, of course, but good stuff that had been made the previous day, stored in a giant commercial refrigerator, and reheated just for you.

I would hire a different chef every day and he'd come back the next day to pass through the dining room and say hello to customers—and hopefully receive some kudos for his work.

I understand the concept of The Leftover Restaurant would not appeal to food snobs—those individuals who haunt upscale restaurants where the dishes have overly creative and misleading names for even the most ordinary foods. You know the ones where whole paragraphs follow the name of the dish, and you are charged enormous sums of money for three average-sized scallops and a wilted string bean leaning across a single spear of asparagus? If you are lucky, there will be a miserly sprig of parsley and a drizzle of something that looks like molasses across it all.

Sorry—I didn't mean to slip over to the dark side of the food industry. Let me regroup.

The Leftover Restaurant could solve one big problem: food waste. According to a report on the CBC, $31 billion worth of food is wasted each year in Canada alone. Not all of that is food that is left on your plate at your local eatery, of course. David Suzuki points out that nearly half of all food produced in the world gets wasted. Maybe properly handled leftovers could help deal with some of that waste.

Maybe? I'm sure of it.

At The Leftover Restaurant, you'd order your food and receive a moderate, but respectable, portion. As the owner of the establishment, I would have a rule: whatever you order, you'd be required to eat at least two vegetables and possibly a salad. You'd be charged more if you didn't order a salad. Heck, the salad would actually be free—and probably fresh, not left over.

Once you cleaned your plate, your server would get you a refill if you liked. You'd be fined a small fee if you left that generous serving of string beans on the plate, of course. Eaters who left more than one sixth of their meal would be banned for life, and once the franchise was in place and successful throughout the world, they would be banned internationally as well.

I guess some customers would find ingenious ways of disposing of those vegetables they didn't want to eat. I am reminded of raising my own two daughters and how they sometimes contrived to avoid eating foods they did not like.

When my daughter Pamela was eight years old, she truly hated broccoli and Swiss chard. She rebelled against these healthy foods for months, and then suddenly relented. This was around the same time many of my socks started disappearing.

She had always been a slow and fussy eater and was often still at the table when the rest of us were getting up to wash dishes and put away the (you guessed it) leftovers. Both daughters had already been apprehended spiriting food they did not like to our dog, Jody, under the table, so the dog was usually sent outside during meals. And then, suddenly, it seemed Pamela had simply given up the food battle and was now eating her greens and broccoli. Battle won. Or not.

A few months later, still anxious to figure out where all my socks had been disappearing to, I started finding them in improbable locations in the woods behind our house. Had they blown there off the laundry line? It seemed unlikely.

It wasn't until Pamela was fifteen that she admitted she had used my stolen socks when she was eight to avoid eating her vegetables. Her tactic had been to deposit the offending food into a sock when my back was turned, tuck the broccoli-laden sock into her pocket, and later throw the hosiery/vegetable package into the forest.

At The Leftover Restaurant, patrons would have to eat their broccoli and Swiss chard. We'd find ways to enforce the rule if necessary. But this leads me to a bit of self-analysis when it comes to how to deal with disliked foods.

My mother made me eat her homegrown, homemade stewed tomatoes. I never did like them, but I ate them. Despite her years of tomato tutelage, I once ate from a can of stewed tomatoes left too long in my fridge (see "Cheez Whiz and Beyond" for the whole story). Not only did the ensuing sickness make a mess of my carpet, but I felt like I was going to die. Revenge of the canned tomato, I suppose. Despite my love affair with leftovers, prudence dictates there is a time limit to how long you keep things, especially anything in a can.

I have tried to maintain an open mind about new and different foods while travelling abroad. My greatest challenge was in Japan when I was commissioned by the Canadian Consulate to give presentations to school kids. I was given the royal treatment as a literary representative of Canada, and one day found myself having a formal lunch with several top officials in the Tokyo government.

I had not been fully informed about the gift-giving ritual that was to take place, and was caught off-guard when one of the mayors (Tokyo has several) presented me with an expensive pen, a plaque, and a glossy photography book. All I had in my pocket was a stick of Juicy Fruit gum, so I bowed deeply and gave him the Juicy Fruit, saying something truly stupid like, "From my people to your people." Fortunately for me, the mayor laughed and graciously accepted the gum, and added that he would like me to join him and his colleagues for karaoke after the meal. I guess he was only joking, though, because there was no karaoke to be had after lunch (which probably saved me more embarrassment).

But the lunch itself was both interesting and challenging. I was given a really cool-looking lacquered wooden box with nearly twenty compartments, each with an item of food more perplexing than the last. I had an interpreter with me, and kept asking her what each new item was as I opened the next drawer.

I recall that many things were variations of fermented soybeans, mushrooms, and sprouts. My hosts anxiously observed me as I tasted each new dish, fumbling with my chopsticks in a manner that caused genial laughter all around the table.

I dutifully swallowed exotic gooey items that smelled most unpleasant to my Western nose, and which thereafter provided a variety of unusual offenses to my taste buds. But I was, after all, representing Canada, and kept diplomacy foremost in my mind. Finally, I came to an item that appeared to look like…well, I can't quite say it, but think of perhaps the worst cold you've ever had in your life—and you'll get the picture.

I asked my interpreter what it was and she had to ask one of the mayors. He answered, but she didn't seem to know how to properly translate the answer. When I asked her again, she told me he'd said no one around the table would be insulted if I declined to taste that item.

I realized the challenge was too great. I could not let my country down. I ate the offending item in one quick swallow to a round of applause and the clicking of many chopsticks, after which my interpreter leaned over, congratulated me, and told me I had just ingested a pickled sea slug.

So, just for the record, there will be no pickled sea slugs on the menu at The Leftover Restaurant—but you will be required to eat your Swiss chard, or there will be hell to pay.

GETTING TO KNOW PATRICK (GETTING TO KNOW NEWFOUNDLAND)

ON AUGUST 18, 2017, PATRICK O'FLAHERTY DIED AT THE AGE of seventy-eight while swimming in Barbour's Pond near Keels in Newfoundland. He was a well-known and well-respected Newfoundland writer, and his passing made me realize we had lost another very important voice from a generation that had grown up in a world so different from the one we live in today.

Because he had shared his stories with me, I felt a bond. I believed I knew the man very well, even though I had never once met him in person, or even talked to him on the phone.

Let me try to explain.

Back in 2014, Patrick sent me the manuscript of his memoir, *Paddy Boy: Growing Up Irish in a Newfoundland Outport*. It was an informative, vivid, opinionated, and edgy story, and I ended up publishing both it and, in 2016, his short story collection, *The Hardest Christmas Ever*. I always feel thrilled and grateful when, as a publisher, I am allowed to bring such illuminating work to the public.

But how could it be that I felt a bond with this particular writer—even though we'd never shaken hands or swapped stories face to face? Heck, I think I even felt a kinship stronger than I have with many people I've known and worked with for years. The reason, of course, is that he so eloquently wrote about his life in the pages of the books. His fiction and his personal history were cut from the same cloth, and his words transported me to a time and place that was almost inconceivable, even though he was little more than a decade older than me.

The son of a fisherman, Patrick grew up in the small coastal community of Long Beach on Conception Bay North, and his memoir covers the years 1939 to 1954. Describing his home village, he writes:

> Very little motor traffic existed in our vicinity. The ratio of people to cars in Newfoundland in 1944 was sixty to one. On the North Shore it may have been two hundred to one. Cows and horses wandered about on roadsides without much fear of being struck by a vehicle. So did sheep and goats.... We had what many outports at this period in Newfoundland history did not have, a road leading to other communities. It was a dusty, muddy, narrow, potholed, sometimes impassable, dirt road, but it was a way out, for those having the means to make full use of it.

In his writing, he took me back to his childhood, the life of a boy growing up in an isolated and unique world of hardship and youthful adventure:

> At Isaac's Cove a liver factory owned by Johnny Johnson, husband of Bridget, still functioned, the last one in Northern Bay. During World War I, prices of ordinary cod oil rose to

unheard-of levels because an ingredient in it was used in explosives, and liver factories in Newfoundland proliferated. Along the shoreline to the Sands, crude wooden ladders led down to beaches and stages. Some whose owners had stopped fishing had fallen into disrepair. You scampered up and down them at your peril. We children became adept at this danger-ous practice, and if a ladder had been removed we climbed down the cliff at the place the ladder had been. Climbing cliffs or moving from cove to cove along the cliff face, maybe a few feet above pounding waves, was great boyish sport.

Through his writing, Patrick reminded me of the very impor-tant role a writer of books still has in this age of frenetic, mostly trivial, yet overwhelming information. He gave us a multi-layered and emotionally infused history of a time and place. He dug deep into the core experience of living in that challenging but exhila-rating time—the feel of it, the stench of the cod liver oil, the dirt under the fingernails from clambering along the cliff—all of it. I'm sure a much tougher childhood could not be found, but somehow, Patrick O'Flaherty made me wish I had been there with him, "a few feet above the pounding waves," on that distant day.

The beauty of memoir writing is that it takes the chaotic ele-ments of everyday life and weaves them together into a wonder-fully large patchwork quilt of images and anecdotes that some-how lets us see that every life has meaning and purpose. Patrick was one of those writers who delivered the goods. As a fiction writer as well, he provided riveting images of the people he knew in real life. In *The Hardest Christmas Ever*, he described an old fisherman thus: "His eyes, pinched from being stung a thousand times by spray from the Atlantic, yet retained a sparkle, for life on the sea keeps a flicker of youth and hope alive even in old men."

I'm fairly certain the author himself maintained that sparkle throughout his life.

The loss of every writer, I believe, is a blow to the community—the writing community for certain—but also to everyone in our region. This is at least partly because, here in Atlantic Canada, our identity is so closely tied to our geography—the land, and especially the sea. In the urban ages to come, this may not be the case. But today, we coastal Canadians are still, to a great degree, shaped by the sea.

The great news is that this author's work lives on. O'Flaherty also wrote a three-volume history of his beloved province titled *Old Newfoundland: A History to 1843*, and *Come Near at Your Peril*, a "candid visitor's guide to the island"—a book so candid, in fact, the provincial government banned it from tourist bureaus (a fact the author was most proud of).

Patrick O'Flaherty was a scholar by trade—a university professor, historian, literary critic (Samuel Johnson was his specialty), and novelist. He was also an editor and journalist, and a man of opinions. He was a mover and shaker, and I expect he stepped on a few toes in his day. He inspired many, and he may have infuriated some.

In *The Pearl*, the community newspaper of Mount Pearl, Burton K. Janes of Bay Roberts wrote:

> *Patrick O'Flaherty has been a mentor of sorts to me for many years. No, I never sat under his teaching as a professor of English at Memorial University. But I have profited immensely from his many books. I return time and again to his* The Rock Observed *as I continue to read the literature of Newfoundland.*

That's the other hat a writer like O'Flaherty wears: mentor. When we read great writers, we learn things from them; we embrace their teachings, absorb their life experiences vicariously, and carry them around in our heads.

My own time in Newfoundland has been limited. It's funny how you can live here in Nova Scotia with that big beckoning island just next door and, more often than not, head off to London, New York, or Paris and forget what exotica lies so close to the north and east of us. I have some limited memories of endless cold rain while hiking in Gros Morne National Park, of a friendly-but-rowdy crowd at The Ship Inn (now The Ship Pub) in St. John's while I was trying to give a poetry reading, and of a hike up to Signal Hill followed by moments of quiet reverie beside the still waters of Quidi Vidi. And I don't think I ever did find a place to buy coffee in Petty Harbour. But that was long ago.

But stories by writers like Patrick O'Flaherty have given me a much richer and deeper understanding of Newfoundland, and I thank him for that. In describing *Paddy Boy*, Patrick once explained to me that he was trying to "get to the pith and substance of that remote world through sense and memory, with history hovering in the background." This is what writers do when they try to make sense of their own past—cull the truly trivial and get to the "pith and substance."

Patrick, I think, reluctantly communicated with me by email. Occasionally, when he had something important to say about the books in progress, his email would read, "I'm sending you a letter that will explain things." And maybe ten days later (the postal service seems extremely slow between Newfoundland and Nova Scotia) I'd receive a handwritten letter in the mail.

The writers of Patrick's generation will be gone soon enough, and I will miss them. While mailing a rare letter myself one snowy winter day, I held open the lid to a postal box on Agricola Street and realized that soon such a ritual will be as archaic as sharpening the nib on a quill pen.

I'll be sure to digitize *Paddy Boy* and *The Hardest Christmas Ever* by the time the snow falls this year. I want to make sure those stories of hard-bitten fishermen and cliff-climbing boys live on for future generations to read via whatever medium they choose.

Going back one more time to his Newfoundland childhood, Patrick writes:

> *Some of my earliest memories are connected to fishing, to boats being built or repaired, salmon nets hanging off fences, cast-net balls, rope everywhere, barking kettles, gasoline casks, fish flakes, the block-and-tackle (pronounced by us taykle), and the like, the tools of my father's trade. He had a wide range of skills, for most work that had to be done in the fishery he had to do himself. He made his own trawls, buoys, moorings, and fittings for his skiff; he could and did build skiffs and dories and make paddles and sculling oars.*

I suppose Patrick O'Flaherty left behind the world of fish for the world of words, and learned well the tools of his trade to enrich our lives with his stories, both real and fictional. His view of his own past and of the history of Newfoundland was by no means sentimental. His was a world of self-reliance and inner strength. And that is what I will most remember him for.

So long, Patrick, and thanks for letting me get to know you.

JUST ANOTHER ORDINARY DAY (ON THE EASTERN SHORE)

I T REALLY WAS JUST ANOTHER ORDINARY DAY ON THE EASTERN Shore of Nova Scotia. Yes—ordinary.

I had just finished fine-tuning a poetry manuscript to be published in the fall. It had one of those fancy, slightly esoteric titles that poetry books sometimes have: *Climbing Knocknarea.* If you don't know the Irish mountain, then it probably doesn't mean much to you, but you should definitely go there some time and climb it, as the title suggests.

The darned publisher had asked me to write three hundred words for the book jacket explaining what the book was about. I puzzled over all sixty or so poems, only to discover they were almost all about ordinary things. Actually, this book was a little more than that. It was a *celebration* of ordinary things. That satisfied me, and the publisher and I realized that much of what I write about is just that. Thus, it was determined I should continue my celebratory efforts by picking a random day and keeping track of the (ordinary) details. So here goes.

On a fine summer day, my dog, Kelty, wakes me up at 6:30 a.m. I leave my wife asleep in bed and go make coffee. Kelty, now one year old comes with me as I drive to the ocean to check the waves and tide. I spill coffee in the driveway as the dog tugs at the leash, hoping to chase after one of our many Arctic hares, one of which still bears his winter coat (we named him Whitey).

There are some small glassy waves at the beach near my house in Lawrencetown. The dog is excited by various creature smells and I'm a little excited about the waves, so I drive the short distance back to my house, put on my wetsuit gear, and head back to the near-empty beach.

There are only a few surfers in the water and one of them is John Allen of Propeller Brewing Co. fame. We trade waves, remark about how cold the water remains in July, and have short discussions about the joys and challenges of the craft beer industry. The waves are maybe three feet high, but the walls are long and smooth and include one particular beauty I will save in my head to reflect on later this month while sitting in the dentist's chair.

After an hour of surfing and the arrival of a crowd of six more surfers, I return home and tell Linda we should drive to Taylor Head Provincial Park, about an hour and a half farther down the Eastern Shore. We throw some food together as the dog gets more and more excited. Then we head east into one of the least-visited but most exotic regions of the province.

So, to get the lay of the land, follow our tour. We pass the big headland on the east end of the beach where I once took my kids sledding in winter—skidding down the monster hill and out onto the ice below. There's Happy Dude's Surf Emporium, with its big smiley sun and sunglasses on the left. We continue on toward Seaforth, where a rather large blue-roofed clam factory has been under construction for several years (a sad monument to some sort of progress in an otherwise idyllic community). Across the street from there is Joe Murphy's house, which I once rented when I first moved to this province. (Once when I jammed and sang with Joe on a version of "Johnny B. Goode" he politely told me that I would do well not to take on a career in music—and he was right, of course.)

We pass the General Store in Grand Desert, currently run by Steve Belfield, and jam-packed with every known commodity. (If you ever run out of guitar picks on your way to Chezzetcook, be sure to stop by.) Next up is the Rose and Rooster. Gourmet coffee in Grand Desert—whodathunkit? But there it is: a friendly café run by Jeff Adams and Sarah Zollinger. The big steeple of Saint Anselm, the West Chezzetcook Catholic church, is up ahead, and across the street they're still tearing down the little carnival sheds built for the recent Chezzetcook Picnic, which has stayed much the same since I first attended in 1976.

As we near the connection to Highway 7 in Porters Lake, the dog, now with his head across my right arm and deeply asleep, looks up as we see the glory of the gleaming white wind turbine that stands behind the grocery store where everyone seems to know my name when I go in to buy yogurt and kale. Wind turbines in this province are a blessing, and I recall a conversation I had with Nova Scotian entrepreneur and philanthropist Charles Keating there in that parking lot in the late 1970s. I was just a hippie living in a shack in West Chezzetcook then, but Charlie and I had a real gabfest about the past, present, and future of Nova Scotia. And Charlie, wherever you are, I hope you can see those spinning blades.

I salute goodbye to the folks at Green Tree Recycling, who have graciously given me a small return on my can and bottle investments, before we hit Highway 7. I thank the green gods of recycling that all my cans and bottles will not end up in a landfill.

It's a quick jaunt down the highway to Musquodoboit Harbour, where I get a whiff of baked goods from Dobbit Bakehouse. Smells like freshly made muffins to me. I see that the library next door is under construction and the historic train is getting rustier by the day. If I were to turn right at this point we'd be headed to Martinique Beach, a five-kilometre sacred stretch of sand, one of the finest ocean beaches the province has to offer.

Then it's over the small gorge of the beautiful Musquodoboit River, on to Smiths Settlement. There's a lively, colourful, revamped bowling alley there called UnBOWLievable Lanes. The crazy artwork on the outside looks like a cross between Haight-Ashbury psychedelic and high-class graffiti—out of place on the Shore, but interesting nonetheless. I suddenly feel remorse that I haven't gone bowling in well over four years due to the closure of Beazley's Lanes back on Main Street. There's gotta be something wrong in the world if people aren't bowling as much. What do we blame? Video games?

We pass through Jeddore and Lake Charlotte where I see that Webber's General Store is now back in business and doing well, and behind that is Memory Lane, which is "an award-winning living history village depicting life in rural Nova Scotia during the 1940s." For them, the '40s were clearly the "good old days," which (to me) is a curious thing, but of course we all need reminders of times past, and the "good old days" can be applied to just about any decade we choose. If you ever have a hankering to see a 1948 International pickup truck or a 1949 Farmall tractor (just like my grandfather had!), that's the place to go.

There are mussel farms in Ship Harbour that have been there

for decades. I've bought bags of their mussels and they're damn good. But I also see a few signs protesting ocean fish farming. The truth is that some fish farms have done serious harm to the environment and wild species of fish. I get it: if you're going to do it, you have to do it right. Fish farms are a big thing of the future, but we have to protect the ocean at all costs.

Most towns along the Eastern Shore don't look like towns at all: Gaetz Brook, Oyster Pond, Ship Harbour, East Ship Harbour, Murphys Cove, Tangier. Folks are friendly and helpful, but they speak of "town," meaning Halifax or Dartmouth, as a place to visit only if you have to—and which you should try to get the heck out of by nightfall. I take a short trip off the main road at the village of Tangier to see what the "Prince Alfred Arch" is. It was built in a small park commemorating a visit in 1861 by, you guessed it, Prince Alfred, son of Queen Victoria, who had a notable military career and who travelled the world allowing British subjects to name streets, schools, and towns after him. He was a great collector of ceramic and glass objects who also loved music, and who once played an out-of-tune violin for dinner guests.

Then Popes Harbour (named for a ship captain, not a pontiff) and Spry Harbour—also named for a sea captain, but a good reminder of my old friend, scholar and literary critic Malcolm Ross, who at ninety told me that he hated it when old people were referred to as "spry." So remember that, youngster, when you're around seniors.

Finally, here comes the turnoff to Taylor Head. The dog is excited as we turn in at the first beach on a chunk of land described by the province as "a rugged windswept peninsula jutting six and a half kilometres into the Atlantic Ocean." "Windswept" is one of those adjectives we writers use to lure unsuspecting tourists to our region. It means something different to those of us who live coastal lives throughout the year. But here, in the middle of July, the sea is becalmed and there is little wind.

The dog explores the length of Bull Beach with us and we keep a good distance from some worried long-beaked shorebirds as they try to keep us well away from their nests. According to the parks folks, the wildlife along the shore around here includes gulls (there are more varieties than you might think), petrels, eiders, scoters, and many kinds of ducks. In the woods and marshes you might run into raccoons, porcupines (don't get me started), white-tailed deer, and muskrats.

Farther out on the peninsula is the amazing Psyche Cove. Psyche is the Greek word for soul and, indeed, this is a most soulful place. It is protected from the outer sea by islands (one of them also named Psyche) so there's no surfing here for me. But it has hard-packed sand and crystal-clear water and a couple of unspoiled kilometres of sheer Nova Scotia coastal beauty to indulge in. On a sunny day, the water has a Caribbean quality—at least until you dip your big toe in. Today there are many jellyfish bobbing about. Psyche Island keeps the sea winds moderated and we picnic on a grassy knoll just off the parking lot. Somehow food tastes better than usual on a day like this.

\But remember, this is just an ordinary day, so we're chilling (in a good way) and taking it easy.

I can't say there was a heck of a lot of excitement on the way home, but we found ourselves dropping by our own beach before retiring for the day. That made me reflect on what bad shape Lawrencetown Beach Provincial Park is in—clearly abandoned by the Department of Natural Resources for unknown reasons. No running water, a deteriorating building, portable toilets instead of bathrooms, torn-up boardwalks—gone and not to be replaced. One of the most-used parks in the province seems to have some kind of curse that has prevented its care and repair. But at least the ocean is still there, and it greets Kelty, Linda, and me with its usual enthusiasm.

Before we leave our final walk on the beach, I take out my camera, thinking, *Yes, the world needs another photo of my little dog.* I get down on my elbows and knees to shoot what I think will be a clever terrier-level image of the dog as he races directly toward me. Unfortunately, he has a nose full of wet sand and he crashes straight into the lens. Later, when I'm inspecting the camera, I discover sand is embedded in the extendable lens and I can't clean it out. So ends the lifespan of a faithful instrument of photography.

I guess every ordinary day truly has its ups and downs.

AUTHOR'S NOTE

MANY OF THESE CHAPTERS ORIGINALLY APPEARED IN THE "NOVA Scotian" section of the *Chronicle Herald*. An earlier version of "Islands of the Heart" was originally part of a speech given at a Nova Scotia Nature Trust fundraiser.